# Introduction

Life is full of challenges and problems; this is one of the things we have to accept that is unavoidable. If you are faced with obstacles, you have to act with perseverance and persistence in order to stay on track with your journey to success and achievement. In order to rise above these obstacles, you will require self-discipline.

If you possess self-discipline, it often leads to building other positive components of yourself, such as self-confidence and self-esteem. Having a good balance of these components in your life leads to higher happiness and satisfaction.

However, if you are lacking self-discipline, it often leads to negative things like failure, health, loss, obesity, relationship problems, and many other undesirable things. Self-discipline is a useful skill that you can learn to overcome negative habits such as; eating disorders, addictions, smoking, and drinking. Everyone requires it in order to develop new skills, self-improvement, meditation, and even spiritual growth.

Like we mentioned above, many people understand all the benefits of having strong self-discipline, but not many actually do the work to develop and strengthen it. Self-discipline is a skill just like any other. You have the ability to strengthen it as long as you keep practicing it. You can specifically focus on building your self-discipline skills through the use of exercises and training.

So why is self-discipline so important and helpful to most people? What can you achieve through strengthening self-discipline? You can achieve most of the goals you set for yourself as long as your mindset is there. Here are all the possible things that self-discipline can help you with:

- Fulfill the promises you make to yourself or other people.

- Avoid acting rashly or impulsively.

- Continue to working on goals even after the initial surge of enthusiasm is gone.

# SELF-DISCIPLINE
# MASTERY

*A Practical Guide to Improve YOUR Self Control, Overcome Failures, Develop Mental Toughness.*

*Learn How to Successfully Achieve YOUR Long-Term Goals the Easy Way.*

**Dalton McKay**

# Table of Contents

Introduction      1

**Chapter 1: A Strong Why for Improving One's Self Discipline**      7

Learned Skill or Innate Characteristic?      9

Will Smith Speech      10

**Chapter 2: Expected Benefits**      **15**

Benefits of Having Self-Discipline      16

**Chapter 3: A Scientific Background**      **25**

Willpower: Changing Your Habits      26

Delaying Gratification      31

Is Willpower a Limited Resource?      36

Emotions vs. Decisions      42

Habits & Willpower Related to Finances      48

The Basal Ganglia and Its Role      51

**Chapter 4: People With High Self-Control Are Happier**      **55**

Habits & Self-Control      56

How Self-Discipline Leads to Increased Happiness      62

How Self-Discipline Affects All Aspects of Your Life      67

**Chapter 5: Failures Are Welcome**      **71**

Edison Mentality      72

Causes of Low Self-Discipline      73

**Chapter 6: The Toolbox**      **85**

Seven Tips to Help You Reach Your Goal of Self-Discipline      85

**Chapter 7: Visualization and Meditation for Personal Growth**                                                   **121**

Visualization is the Key to Improved Performance          123

How Worries Are Reprogramming Your Brain               126

Positive Visualization Techniques                        130

Using Meditation to Achieve Your Goals                   140

**Chapter 8: Master Self-Discipline**                         **149**

Next Level Tips                                          149

Dealing With Setbacks and Develop a Growth Mindset       155

The Final Challenge: Achieve Your Long Term Goals        159

**Conclusion**                                                **165**

- Going to the gym or getting exercise despite your mind telling you to stay home and watch TV instead.

- Overcoming procrastination and laziness.

- Continue working on your diet and constantly fighting the urge to eat unhealthy foods.

- Waking up early in the morning.

- Meditating regularly.

- Start reading a book and finishing it.

- Overcoming bad habits like watching too much TV.

In order for you to strengthen your self-discipline, you may find it easier if you make the effort to behave and act in accordance with the decisions or goals you make despite the tendency to procrastinate, desire to give up, and general laziness.

Throughout this book, you will be learning about different ways that you can achieve self-discipline through. Popular techniques include visualization and meditation.

These are techniques that people use to envision themselves achieving the goals and success that they want in life. By being able to picture what they want, people have achieved goals that they never thought were possible simply by altering their mindset and overcoming bad habits.

People such as athletes and entrepreneurs all rely heavily on their self-discipline ability in order to achieve the success that they want. You can strengthen your self-discipline, even if it's weak, by simply exercising your self-discipline muscle, which you can practice anywhere and anytime.

The way that this book is structured is to help you learn what self-discipline actually is and how it manifests within us before we get into the practical exercises. You will be learning all the behind the scenes effects and benefits that self-discipline will bring and some challenges that you will face along the way. You will be learning different techniques and hearing some stories of successful people who used self-discipline to accomplish their goals.

These techniques have been thoroughly studied by multiple professionals in the field of psychology. There are numerous published books, studies, and articles that have found a plethora of evidence that supports the effectiveness of these techniques. Take these techniques seriously and try to actually exercise it in your life. Many people tend to just finish reading a book but don't actually begin any of the exercises or build the mindsets that are recommended.

So, no matter how young or old, how inexperienced or experienced, or how much education level you have, this book will be able to help you strengthen your self-discipline so you can utilize it in your daily life to achieve the things you want to achieve. The things you want to achieve don't have to be huge goals like building your own billion-dollar company, but you can use it to start achieving some little things that you want in life.

This can be quitting smoking, eating healthier, or completing a personal project that's important to you. Regardless of who you are and what you want to accomplish, the basis of self-discipline is the same for everyone. This book will help you understand everything you need to know about self-discipline, the benefits, and challenges that it brings, and I will provide you with a step by step process on how you can achieve self-discipline along with some practical exercises that you can use to strengthen it.

Don't wait any longer, begin this journey and start achieving all the goals that you've always wanted to achieve.

# Chapter 1: A Strong Why for Improving One's Self Discipline

Self-discipline is one of the most useful and vital skills that everyone will benefit from having. This skill is crucial in pretty much every area of a person's life. Although most people know how important this skill is, not many take the time to practice strengthening it. The common belief regarding self-discipline is living a strict and limited lifestyle while being harsh to oneself. However, self-discipline simply means self-control and building the inner strength to control yourself, your behavior, and your reactions.

Self-discipline is the power that a person has in order to be able to stick with their decisions and to follow them through without changing their minds. This is one of the most important conditions before one can achieve their goals. Having self-discipline allows people to persevere with their decisions and continues to plan to accomplish their goals. Self-discipline can also be known as inner strength, which helps people overcome obstacles like laziness, procrastination and even addictions.

One of the main traits of self-discipline is the ability to deny instant gratification and pleasure in return for greater gain, which requires a person to put in effort and time to achieve. Most people know that self-discipline is one of the most crucial components when it comes to success. Here is how self-discipline expresses itself:

- Self-control.

- Perseverance.

- The ability to not give up even when faced with obstacles and failure.

- The ability to resist temptations or distractions.

- The ability to keep trying until you accomplish the goal you've set.

# Learned Skill or Innate Characteristic?

Self-Discipline is a learned skill. It is not an innate characteristic. What does this mean? I will start by defining these two terms for you. A learned skill, as I am sure you can imagine, is something that you can learn and develop in order to possess. This is the opposite of an innate characteristic, which is something that you are born with. There are some characteristics that you are born with such as the color of your eyes or certain aspects of your personality such as being stubborn or brave.

The other difference is that one is a skill, and the other is a characteristic. Skills are things that you can study, practice and improve upon. Skills are things like communication or cooking. A characteristic is something that you possess that you do not have much control over. You can work on things like becoming braver, but for the most part, you are born a brave person or you are not.

Knowing this fact can help you to feel empowered and hopeful. If you struggle with self-discipline, knowing that it is a skill that can be learned and honed over time means that this will not remain something that you struggle with anymore. By reading this book, you are already taking the first steps to changing your life by becoming a more self-disciplined person. If this were an innate characteristic, this would mean that it would be difficult for you to change.

## Will Smith Speech

Will Smith once gave a motivational speech in which he talked about discipline. He said that often, people think of the word discipline as something negative, like when you have to discipline a child or when you punish yourself for not being disciplined enough. He went on to say that discipline should not be thought of in this negative sense, but instead, we should take the punishment out of it and think of it as a choice.

Discipline is a choice within oneself that is a decision to forego current satisfaction or reward in order to have long-term benefits or self-respect. In this way, self-discipline is not something that involves learning through punishment, but instead, it is something that involves waiting for future benefits. Instead of punishing, you are proving the benefits of this to yourself by seeing the positive results that it produces for you in the future.

This means that when we teach children about discipline, we are not punishing them in order to teach them how to conduct themselves, we are showing them that if they can forego instant gratification, they will see long-term rewards in the future that come in the form of positive benefits and, as a result, a higher level of self-respect.

In his speech, Will Smith also connects self-discipline with self-love. He says that self-discipline and self-love are deeply connected to one another. That when practicing and employing self-love, you are doing so by having self-discipline. Therefore, in order to achieve self-love, you must learn the skill of self-discipline. This further solidifies the point that I mentioned above, about self-discipline being a skill and not an innate characteristic, since self-love is not an innate characteristic.

Since self-discipline results in more self-respect over time, this is how it leads to the development and practice of self-love. Self-discipline is a loving act toward oneself since you are choosing what is best for yourself in the long-run instead of in the present moment only. He says that people often base their opinion of themselves on other people's perception of them, but that the problem with this is that other people should have no effect on how we feel about ourselves.

Since self-discipline is self-love, we should only be concerned with our level of self-discipline when determining how we feel about ourselves or our self-esteem. If you can look at yourself and your choices and say that you were practicing self-discipline, then you will feel more self-love, and therefore, you will have a higher level of self-esteem.

Will Smith also related self-discipline to taking responsibility. He said that being able to take responsibility for things is related to self-discipline. For example, if your partner cheats and leaves the marriage, it is up to you to take responsibility for yourself by going forward and deciding how you are going to make a good life for yourself without them. Of course, this is very hard to do. The tendency would often be to focus on the other person and how they hurt you and how they are at fault. While this all may be true, it does not help you in the long-run to think of this over and over.

The only thing that helps you in the long-run is to exercise self-discipline in order to get up, take responsibility for yourself and your own life, and make decisions for a better future. You may feel better in the moment if you focus on how they are at fault and how they wronged you, but this is not what self-disciplined people do. This is what is called the victim mindset. By allowing yourself to stay in this victim mindset for too long, you are allowing your ex-partner to control your life instead of taking control of it yourself.

By being a person who takes responsibility, this leads to more self-respect and higher self-esteem because of the long-term benefits that they earned through handling the situation in a self-disciplined manner. Nobody else can be responsible for your happiness or your decisions, and this cannot be taken lightly. Approaching every decision from this angle will help you to feel empowered and in control of your life.

# Chapter 2: Expected Benefits

In order to get yourself committed to strengthening your self-discipline, you must understand what the expected benefits are. Learning the benefits should help you get an idea of all the goals you want to accomplish, which will act as a catalyst for you to stay committed to your 30-day plan. The benefits that come with strengthening your self-discipline ranges from improving your relationships all the way to increase your overall success.

Despite what your goals are, self-discipline is something that can help you improve multiple areas of your life. We will also talk about some of the causes of low self-discipline in chapter 5. By learning what the common causes are, you can identify them within yourself. Let's take a look at some of the benefits first.

# Benefits of Having Self-Discipline

When a person has strong self-discipline, it leads to higher self-regard, inner strength, self-assurance, and ultimately to satisfaction and happiness. It leads to better outcomes in every area of a person's life. This includes gaining more personal, business, and relationship success. The following benefits of self-discipline are ones that may not automatically come to mind.

## Benefit #1: Self Discipline Creates Inner Strength and Character

According to a famous psychology book, there was an important statement that the author wrote. He stated that everyone is the person that they wish to be. All that is stopping you from behaving in the manner that you want to behave is your emotional mind. Let's think about that for a second. Although you may be a very kind and caring person, if you have a tendency to lose your temper easily, other people may see you as a hothead or an angry person.

In this example, you don't necessarily need to change who you are as a person. Instead, you need to change the way you behave. Once you change the way you behave, other people will then see you for the person that you truly are. For example, you already are that kind and caring person, but your short temper is preventing you from showing that personality to the world. Self-discipline is a tool that can help you to stop acting on your impulses and instead act based on your true character.

By creating more inner strength and character, you will be able to better focus on your goals and build more persistence when you are faced with obstacles. Practicing self-discipline can help grow your inner strength and character.

## Benefit #2: Self-Discipline Allows You to Resist Temptations

As we discussed in chapter one, our modern-day lives are filled to the brim with temptations that can throw people off track and prevent them from achieving their goals. Often, these temptations are temporary, and by exercising willpower, most people can overcome the urge. In our modern workplace, temptations tend to take the form of distractions like checking your phone, a conversation at the water cooler, or scrolling through social media.

Those examples are just the tip of the iceberg when it comes to our modern-day potential distractions. When you are able to recognize what your temptations are, you can place a strategy in order to resist them. This requires less self-discipline compared to ignoring the temptation with brute mental force. For example, if your coworker locks her phone in the drawer of her desk and refuses to check her phone during the workday. She may make this strategy easier for her by telling all of her friends that she does this so that her friends do not expect an immediate response.

As we already learned, temptations also exist in the form of addictions and bad habits. When self-discipline is coupled with effective strategies, it is a very valuable tool that can be used to overcome most urges in life.

## Benefit #3: Stronger Self-Discipline Increases One's Chances of Success

When a goal can be achieved with great ease, some would argue whether or not it should even be considered a goal. Goals require a person to stretch and grow; to improve skills, attitudes, and to improve one's knowledge. When an individual meets those requirements, they improve the quality of their life along with improving their capability to take on larger and harder challenges. Ultimately, goals should be challenging.

Everyone will face barriers and obstacles in which they would need to overcome. This is the action that is needed in order to create personal growth. In order to overcome these obstacles and barriers to achieve your goals, it will require a lot of self-discipline and self-belief. A person's ability to persevere and overcome obstacles when faced with difficulty is often times the difference between failure and success.

Self-discipline helps increase your success due to the fact that it will help you overcome obstacles. Most people give up on their goals when they are confronted with a problem. Self-discipline encourages stronger problem-solving skills, better organization, and more efficient time management. By strengthening those skills, you naturally become a better leader that will help you earn more money in your career.

## Benefit #4: People With Self-Discipline Build Better Relationships

Take a minute to think about some of the things that you value in a relationship. This could be a friendship, a romantic relationship, or a familial relationship. You may value important things like integrity, dependability, loyalty, and honesty. All of these traits require a person to have a strong character. It requires someone who is able to be true and act true to their values and beliefs, even when it would be easier to fall into temptation.

As we already discussed, those with self-discipline are more likely to develop a stronger character. They have a lot of practice in doing the things that they know need to be done, even though they would probably rather be doing something else. Generally, they are a person that most people can count on. They are more effective when it comes to gaining respect and building trust amongst their peers.

Self-discipline can help you build better relationships by allowing you to have a better peace of mind. This will help foster marriages, relationships with your children, and even help you stay physically active. If you are able to maintain a healthy body, you will have more energy to help you accomplish your goals and commit to them.

*If you are interested in improving your communication skills and building effective interpersonal work relationships, I wrote a book on the subject that you can find on Amazon. Go to the last page of this book and you will find the direct link.*

## Benefit #5: Self-Discipline Makes It More Difficult for a Person to Be Offended

People with more self-discipline tend to be calmer, assured, and more confident. They know who they are as a person and what they believe in. They will always do what they believe to be the right thing. As we mentioned throughout this book, although the task that needs to be done may not be something that they want to do at that very moment in time, the strength of self-discipline demands them to be true to their values and beliefs. One of the major benefits of this behavior of a self-disciplined person is that they can always be confident that they have done their best.

If a person knows that they tried their very best and couldn't have done any better, they will be able to hold their heads up high, knowing that any insults or criticism are meaningless. However, this person would also be prepared to listen to any constructive criticism but negative feedback does not affect them much at all. To maximize the benefits of self-discipline, a person must have goals that are effective in motivating and inspiring them.

Photo by <u>Brooke Lark</u> on <u>Unsplash</u>

# Chapter 3: A Scientific Background

Understanding what the psychology behind self-discipline it is extremely crucial as it will help you learn what the driving factors are behind it. One of the main factors that drive self-discipline is willpower. A common belief in people is that they think they can change their lives for the better if they simply could just have more willpower. Charles Duhigg is a prize-winning author who covers the subject of 'The Power of Habit'. In this chapter, we will talk about similar topics related to his book regarding how willpower is not as needed if you are able to develop habits.

If people had more willpower, everyone would be able to save responsibly for retirement, exercise regularly, stop procrastinating, avoid alcohol and drugs, and achieve all kinds of their noble goals. One survey that studied all Americans and their annual stress found that the majority of the participants reported that lacking willpower is the number one reason for not following the changes that they want for themselves. In order for a person to be able to change their daily routine and habits, they must have enough willpower to do so.

## Willpower: Changing Your Habits

In the survey that we just mentioned, it was reported that the biggest obstacle when it comes to people achieving change was the lack of willpower. Even though many people often place blame upon the scarcity of their willpower for their unhealthy choices, they are still grasping on to the hope of being able to achieve it one day. Most people in this study also reported that they think willpower is something that can be taught and learned. They are absolutely correct. Some research recently has discovered many ways of how willpower can be strengthened with training and practice.

On the contrary, some participants in the survey expressed that they think they would have more willpower if they had more free time to spare. However, the concept of willpower isn't something that increases automatically if a person has more time in their day. So that leads me to the next question, how can people resist when they are faced with temptation? Over the last several years, many discoveries were made about how willpower works by scientists all over the world. We will dive a little deeper into what our current understanding of willpower is.

Weak willpower isn't the only reason for a person to fail at achieving their goals. Psychologists in the field of willpower have built three crucial components when it comes to achieving goals. They said that you first need to set a clear goal and then establish the motivation for change. They said the second component was to monitor your behavior in regards to that goal. Willpower itself is the third and final component. If your goal is similar to the following; stop smoking, get fit, study more, or stop wasting time on the internet, willpower is an important concept to understand if you are looking to achieve any of those goals.

The bottom line of willpower is the ability to achieve long term goals by resisting temporary temptations and urges. Here are several reasons why this is beneficial. Over the course of a regular school year, psychologists performed a study that examined the self-control in a class of eighth-grade students. The researchers in this study did an initial assessment of the self-discipline within the students by getting the students, their parents and teachers to fill out a questionnaire.

They took it one step further and gave these students a task of deciding whether they want to receive $1 right away or $2 if they waited a week. At the end of the study, the results pointed to the fact that the students that had better test scores, better school attendance, better grades, and had a higher chance of being admitted to competitive high school programs all ranked high on the self-discipline assessment. These researchers found that self-discipline played a bigger role than IQ when it came to predicting academic success.

Other studies have found similar evidence. In a different study, researchers asked a group of undergraduate university students to fill out self-discipline questionnaires that will be used to assess their self-control. These researchers developed a scale that helped score the student's in relation to the strength of their willpower. They found that the students that had higher self-esteem, better relationship skills, higher GPA, and had less alcohol or drug abuse all had the highest self-control scores from the questionnaire.

Another study found that the benefits of willpower tend to be relevant well past university years. This self-control study was conducted in a group of 1000 people who had been tracked since birth to the age of 32. This is a long term study in New Zealand, where they wanted to learn more about the effects of self-control well into adulthood. They found that the people who had high self-control during their childhood grew up into adults that had better mental and physical health.

They also had fewer substance abuse problems, criminal convictions, better financial security, and better money-saving habits. These patterns were proven even after the researchers had adjusted external influences such as socioeconomic factors, general intelligence, and these people's home lives. These findings prove why willpower is extremely important in almost all areas of a person's life.

Now that you have learned the importance of willpower and the role it plays in multiple stages of a person's life, let's define it a little further. There are many other names used for willpower that is used interchangeably. This includes; drive, determination, self-control, resolve, and self-discipline. Some psychologists will characterize willpower in even more specific ways. Some define willpower to be:

- The capacity to overcome unwanted impulses, feelings, or thoughts.

- The ability to resist temporary urges, temptation and delay instant gratification in order to achieve goals that are more long-term.

- The effortful and conscious regulation of oneself.

- The ability to engage a "cool" cognitive system of behavior rather than a "hot" emotional system.

- A limited resource that has the capability to be depleted.

## Delaying Gratification

Over 40 years ago, there was a research project that studied self-control within children using a simple and effective test. You may have seen this study used before in modern-day experiments. His experiment is called the "marshmallow test". This test has become extremely famous over the years as it laid the groundwork and then paved the way for modern studies of self-control.

This psychologist and his colleagues began the test by showing a plate of marshmallows to a child at the preschool age. Then, the psychologist let the child know that he had to go outside for a few moments and that he would let the child make a very simple decision. If the child could wait until the psychologist came back into the room, she could have two marshmallows. If the child could not or doesn't want to wait, then she can ring the bell which then the psychologist would come back to the room right away but then she would only get to have one marshmallow.

Willpower can be defined as simple as the ability for a person to delay instant gratification. Children who have high self-control are able to give up the immediate gratification of eating a marshmallow so that they can be able to eat two of them at a later time. People who have quit smoking sacrifice the satisfaction of one cigarette in hopes of having better health and lower the risk of cancer in the future. Shoppers fight the urge to spend money at a mall so they can save their money for their future retirement. You probably get the point here.

This marshmallow experiment actually helped the researchers develop a framework that explains people's ability to resist or delay instant gratification. He proposed a system that he calls "hot and cool" in order to explain whether willpower will succeed or fail. The 'cool' system is naturally a cognitive one. It means that it is a thinking system that uses knowledge about feelings, sensations, goals, and actions that remind oneself, for example, why the marshmallow shouldn't be eaten.

The cool system is very reflective, while the hot system is more emotional and impulsive. The hot system is responsible for quick and reflex-based responses to specific triggers, for example, eating the single marshmallow without thinking about the long term ramifications. To put this in layman's terms, if this framework were a cartoon, the hot system would be the devil and the cool system would be the angel on your shoulder.

When somebody's willpower fails, their hot system essentially overrides their cool system, which leads them to make impulsive actions. However, some people are more or less affected by the hot system triggers. That susceptibility to emotional responses plays a big role in influencing a person's behavior throughout life.

The same researcher discovered that when he revisited his experiment with the children that had now grown up into adolescents, he found that the teenagers who were able to wait longer to have two marshmallows when they were children were more likely to have higher SAT grades and their parents were more likely to rate them of having better ability to handle stress, plan, respond to reason and exhibit self-control in frustrating situations and could concentrate better without being easily distracted.

Funnily enough, the marshmallow study didn't end there. A few other researchers tracked down almost 60 people who are now middle-aged, who had previously been a part of the marshmallow experiment as young children. These psychologists proceeded to test the participants' willpower strength using a task that's been proven to prove self-control within adults. Surprisingly, the participants' various willpower strengths had been very consistent over the last 40 years.

Overall, they found that the children who were not successful in resisting the first marshmallow did poorly on the self-control tasks as an adult and that their hot stimuli seem to be consistent throughout their lifetime. They also began to study brain activity in some of the participants by using magnetic resonance technology. When these participants were presented with tempting stimuli, those who had low willpower exhibited brain patterns that were very different from the brain patterns of those that had strong willpower.

They discovered that the prefrontal cortex (this is the region of the brain that controls choice-making functions) was more active in the participants who had stronger willpower and the ventral striatum (an area of the brain that is focused on processing rewards and desires) showed increased activity in the participants who had weaker willpower.

## Is Willpower a Limited Resource?

The hot-cold framework does a great job of explaining people's ability to delay gratification but there is another theory that is called 'willpower depletion' that has emerged in recent years to explain what happens to people after they have resisted multiple temptations. Everyone exerts willpower every day in one form or another.

People resist to surf the web or go on social media instead of finishing their work report. They may choose a salad when they are craving a slice of pizza. They may hold their tongue rather than make a snide remark. Recent growing research indicates that resisting temptations repeatedly takes a mental toll on a person. Some people describe willpower as a muscle that can get tired if overused.

The earliest discoveries of this concept came from a study that was conducted in Germany. The researcher brought participants into a room that smelled like fresh-baked cookies. The participants sat down at the table that held a bowl of radishes and a plate of those freshly baked cookies. The researchers asked some of the participants to taste those cookies while the others were asked to try the radishes.

After this, the participants were assigned to complete a difficult geometric puzzle in 30 minutes. The researchers found that the participants who had to eat the radishes (therefore resisting the urge to eat the cookies) took 8 minutes to give up on the puzzle while the participants who got to eat the cookies tried to complete the puzzle for 19 minutes. The evidence here seems as if the people who used their willpower to resist eating the cookies drained their resources for future situations.

In the late 90s, this research was published, and since then, numerous other studies have begun looking into willpower depletion or otherwise known as ego depletion. One study, for example, the participants were asked to hold back and suppress any feelings they had while they watched an emotional film. These participants then participated in a physical stamina test but gave up sooner than the participants who watched the movie and reacted normally without any suppression.

Depleting willpower is very common in today's society. You have probably tried to make yourself be diplomatic when you are dealing with an aggravating customer or forced to fake happiness when your in-laws come to stay with you for an extended period of time. You must have realized that certain social interacts demand the use of willpower. There is also existing research that has proven that people interacting with others and maintaining relationships often is a high depleter of willpower.

Willpower depletion is not solely just a simple case of feeling tired. During another study by the same researcher, she had the participants in her study go through a whole day of sleep deprivation and then asked them to watch a movie but to suppress their emotions and reactions during it. She then proceeded to test the strength of the participant's self-control and found that those participants who didn't get sleep were not much more likely to be depleted of willpower compared to those who got a full night's sleep.

So if willpower isn't related to physical fatigue, then what exactly is it? Research studies recently have discovered a few different mechanisms that are possibly responsible for willpower depletion, some that were at the biological level. The researchers found that the people whose willpower became depleted after completing self-control tasks showed lowered activity in the region of their brain that controlled cognition. When willpower is being tested, a person's brain may begin to function differently.

Some other evidence indicates that people who have depleted willpower might be on low on fuel quite literally. Since the brain is an organ that requires high-energy that is powered by glucose, certain professionals suggested that the cells in the brain that are responsible for maintaining a person's self-control use up glucose quicker than it is being replenished. They performed a study with dogs, where the dogs that were obedient and were asked to resist temptation showed lower blood glucose levels compared to the dogs that did not need to use self-control.

They found similar patterns in humans during scientific studies. The people who needed to use willpower in tasks were tested to have lower glucose levels compared to the participants that weren't asked to utilize their willpower. Moreover, replenishing glucose levels tend to help reboot a depleted willpower source in individuals that were depleted while drinking a sugar-free drink did not.

However, there is still evidence that suggests that the depletion of willpower can be maintained by a person's attitudes and beliefs. Different research and other colleagues found out that the people who felt the need to use their willpower (usually in order to please other people) were found to be more easily depleted compared to the people who are driven by their own desires and goals. These researchers, therefore, suggested that the people who are in better touch with themselves may be better off in life compared to the people who are often people-pleasing.

Some other researchers also studied how the effects of mood could affect a person's willpower. A study that took place in 2010 discovered that the group of people who believed that willpower is a resource that is limited were more likely to have willpower depletion. However, the group of people that did not believe that willpower can be depleted didn't show any symptoms or signs of willpower exhaustion after using their self-control.

During the next stage of the same study, the psychologists manipulated the participant's subconscious beliefs by getting them to unknowingly fill out a biased questionnaire. The group that was manipulated to believe that willpower is for a fact a limited resource exhibited symptoms of willpower depletion/exhaustion while the group that believed that willpower was not depletable didn't show any signs of declining self-control.

So at the end of all this evidence and discussion, do you think willpower is a limited resource? Many ideas point to evidence that supports both spectrums of this answer. They argued that willpower depletion in the early stages can be buggered by factors such as belief and mood. However, more research is definitely required for us to explore how moods, attitudes, and beliefs might be affecting a person's ability to resist temptation.

## Emotions vs. Decisions

A person makes decisions every day in order to resist urges and gratification so that they can seek a more healthy and happy long term life. This could be in the form of refusing another portion of fries, forcing yourself to go work out, denying the second round of alcoholic drinks, or overcoming the temptation to skip early morning meetings. Willpower within everyone is being tested on a constant basis.

Lack of willpower is often known as the main obstacle to people's ability to maintain a healthy weight and physique. A lot of research actually supports this idea. A study found that children that had better self-control had less likelihood of becoming overweight when they grew up into their adolescence years due to their ability to delay gratification and control their urges.

However, just like we talked about earlier, resisting those urges may diminish a person's willpower to resist the next temptation. A researcher proved this in a study where they offered students that were currently dieting some ice cream after watching a sad movie. Some of the participants were asked to watch the movie like any other normal day while the other group was asked to not show any reactions or emotions, which is a task that requires self-control.

The psychologists discovered that the participants who had to use their self-control to withhold their emotions and reactions indulged in more ice cream compared to the participants who were allowed to watch the movie normally and react as they'd like.

A lot of people often place most of the blame on their bad moods for causing their 'emotional eating'. However, that study found that the participants' emotional states were not the cause of the amount of ice cream that they consumed. In layman's terms, the depletion of willpower had more significance than a person's mood when it comes to determining how much ice cream the participants ate.

We have to keep in mind that the reason behind why someone is on a diet will also play a role in willpower depletion. As we had just discussed, researchers found that people's attitudes and inner beliefs may create a buffer for them in terms of the effects of willpower depletion. In a further example that this based off this theory, the researchers asked participants to resist the temptation of eating cookies that were placed in front of them.

He then tested the participant's strength of self-control by getting them to squeeze an exercise handgrip until they couldn't anymore He discovered through this exercise that the people who refused to eat the cookies for their own reasons (such as finding enjoyment in resisting treats) showed better control in this physical test compared to the ones who refused the cookies for reasons that were external (wanting to impress the experimenter).

At this point, it is obvious that willpower is a required component when it comes to eating healthy. If a person is living in a surrounding where there were plenty of unhealthy but delicious food options, the action of resisting temptation is more likely to deplete willpower and even making it difficult for highly motivated healthy eaters. Since the behaviors of overeating are very complex, the role of willpower is argumentative when it comes to discussions for obesity treatments.

Some of the experts in the field of willpower believe that using self-control and personal choices causes people to be stigmatized, which makes them unlikely to be motivated to lose weight. Many dieticians advise against using willpower as a tool and argue that dieters should be focusing on lowering the effect that their environment will have on their eating habits and behavior.

Ultimately, when it comes to the world we live in today, resisting the temptation to eat unhealthily can be a hard challenge. We are constantly exposed to ads for delicious high-calorie foods. Cheap and fast processed foods are available at our fingertips 24/7 and are less expensive compared to healthier options. A person's willpower and the environment that they live in plays a big role in people's choices when it relates to food. Having a better understanding of both of these elements will help individuals and dieticians that are battling obesity.

Not only does willpower play a role in eating healthy, but it also plays a role in the use and possible abuse of alcohol, tobacco, and drugs. Children who have developed self-control may avoid substance abuse in their adulthood and teenagehood. Researchers in this field studied the self-control of adolescents as they moved from sixth grade to eleventh grade. They discovered that the kids who had problems with self-control in sixth grade, such as not speaking in turn during class, had more likelihood of using tobacco, marijuana, and alcohol as high schoolers.

This may not come as surprising, but willpower also plays a significant role in curbing alcohol abuse and usage. In another study, a researcher discovered that people who drank socially very often that used their willpower during the lab proceeded to go out and consume more alcohol compared to the other participants who didn't use their willpower stockpile.

In a different study, the researcher found that the social drinkers who had used a lot of their self-control that day were more likely to infringe on the drinking limits that they created for themselves. This finding shows evidence that exerting self-control excessively in one situation can cripple a person's ability to fight off other temptations in different parts of their life.

We are talking a lot about willpower because understanding the role that it plays is very important for developing effective treatments and plan to battle serious issues like addictions to help guide people in making healthier choices for themselves. Willpower research offers people lots of suggestions on how to stick with healthy behaviors.

## Habits & Willpower Related to Finances

The temptation of consuming in materialistic things like new shoes or a new car is a test of willpower that we have all experienced. Just like how unhealthy food options have become plentiful, the opportunities for impulse spending has grown as well. ATMs are on every corner, and the rise of shopping online only allows a person to spend all their money without having to even leave the comfort of their couch. Willpower depletion affects people's ability to

48

choose healthier lifestyle options and also affects their purchasing behavior.

Professors from the University of Minnesota did a study that focused on impulse buying and willpower depletion. They showed the participants a silent movie with a series of words that appeared on the bottom of the screen. A group of those participants was asked not to pay attention to those words, which were a task that required the use of self-control. After the movie, the participants were asked to look through a catalog with products like cars and watches and they wrote down the money amount that they were willing to pay for every single item.

The participants that used self-control during the movie were willing to spend more money, about $30,000, while the participants who didn't deplete their willpower were willing to spend approximately $23,000.

In the next experiment, the researchers tested the spending behavior of the participants by showing them the opportunity to buy lower-cost objects like cups and decorative stickers. The group that had done self-control in the previous experiment expressed that they felt a higher temptation to buy those items. In fact, they purchased more items and spent more money compared to the participants who hadn't done the self-control exercise. The task of making financial decisions can be much harder for people that are impoverished.

Researchers conducted various studies in India to explore the relationship between poverty and will power strength. In one study, this researcher visited two different Villages one that was poor and one that was richer. The researcher offered people an opportunity to buy a luxury brand name soap at an extremely discounted price tag. This item was a great deal in terms of cost but it still showed that people who live in poverty had difficulty making financial decisions as such.

The participants in the study were told to squeeze a handgrip made for exercise, which is a popular test of strength regarding self-control, before and after the soap was offered to be purchased. The researcher found that the participants who had more money exercised the handgrip for the same amount of time prior and post the opportunity to buy that soap.

However, they found that poor participants squeezed the handgrip for a smaller amount of time after making a purchasing decision. Their willpower was depleted, and the researcher had concluded that it was likely run down by the difficulty of making that financial decision.

## The Basal Ganglia and Its Role

Now that we've learned about willpower, habits, and decision-making, let's talk a little bit about the psychology and science behind it. Our brain consists of different areas that have different jobs when it comes to our reasoning abilities. One of the areas is called the basal ganglia, and it's responsible for controlling our routine habits and behaviors. Our prefrontal cortex is responsible for our decision making. When a person makes a prefrontal cortex decision that isn't in line with our habitual basal ganglia behavior, you're going to feel a bit weird and out of place.

For instance, let's say that you have a bad habit of going to bed late at night, say 2 am and onwards. One of the goals that you plan on achieving through self-discipline is to go to bed earlier, let's say you will aim for midnight. When you first start to use discipline to make yourself be in bed by 12 am, it's going to feel wrong and unnatural. You'll likely feel the temptation to go back to your bad habits. You might want to get up from bed and watch some television or scroll through your phone mindlessly in bed until 2 am.

In order to get your basal ganglia to work with your prefrontal cortex, you must build the habit. To build habit, you must commit to doing that action repeatedly until it no longer feels unnatural to you. At this point, you actually stop exerting your willpower and you are acting on pure habit alone. What this means is that you no longer need to use self-discipline to achieve that goal as your habits are doing it for you on autopilot.

The trick to moving past the unnatural feeling when you are first beginning to build a new habit is to look at what that action will do for you and do not look at it from how it feels in the moment. You already know that this action you are trying to change will feel unnatural in the beginning, but reminding yourself that you are doing it to achieve a long-term goal will help you move past the beginning stages of feeling unnatural.

When you repeat this action for the second, third, fourth, fifth, or more times, it will slowly turn into a habit and it will feel natural to you. This is when your prefrontal cortex and basal ganglia are in tune with each other.

# Chapter 4: People With High Self-Control Are Happier

In this chapter, we will be learning about self-control, habits, and how people that have higher self-control tend to live happier lives. Those who have self-control have the ability to delay gratification and see the long term benefits of their goals. If a person does not have goals, or has them but has no motivation to ever achieving them, then they are more likely to live a life that is stagnant and unfulfilling. However, achieving your goals doesn't have to be something where you utilize your willpower every day.

When you are able to turn the necessary action items that will help you achieve your goals into a habit, you no longer need to draw from your willpower resources. When an action becomes a habit, it becomes a part of your auto-pilot routine that kicks into gear when it is called for. We will first learn about the relationship between habits and self-control and then move onto the two subchapters that will teach you how self-discipline can increase your happiness and can positively impact all areas of your life.

## Habits & Self-Control

A ton of research has been developed recently in order to explain the numerous elements of willpower. Many professionals that study this area of self-control to this with one goal on their mind. They are about these types of questions: If willpower is a limited resource, what can we do to conserve it? How can we strengthen willpower?

One effective tactic for maintaining willpower is simply to avoid temptation. In the marshmallow study, children were given a choice of being allowed to eat one marshmallow right away or having to wait an undefined period of time to have the opportunity to eat two marshmallows.

They found that the kids who started at the marshmallows during the whole time were found to be less likely to resist the treat compared to the kids who shut their eyes and refused to look, looked away, or created a distraction for themselves. The technique of out of sight, out of mind, works with adults as well. In a recent study, researchers found that office workers who kept unhealthy snacks such as candy in their desk drawers consumed it less compared to when they would put the candy on top of their desks at eye level.

A technique called **"implementation intention"** is another helpful tactic that helps improve willpower. These intentions are usually in the form of "if-then" statements that aid people in planning for situations that are likely to disrupt their goals.

For instance, a person that is monitoring their consumption of alcohol may tell themselves before entering a drinking party that if anybody offers them an alcoholic drink, then they will request a plain soda with lime. Research has found that amongst adults and adolescents, implementing solutions will increase self-control, even if people already had their willpower depleted by other tasks. People that have a plan ahead of time allows them to easily make decisions at the moment without needing to draw upon their bank of willpower resources.

This research suggests that people have a bank of willpower that is limited and that raises a few troubling questions. Are people destined to fail if they are being faced with too many temptations? The answer is not necessarily. Many psychologists have the belief that a person's willpower cannot be ever used up completely. Instead, people often have stored some back-up willpower that is being saved for future demands. Those reserves are only available for the right type of motivation, allowing them to accomplish things even when their willpower has seemingly run out.

In order to demonstrate this idea, a researcher further found out that individuals who had their willpower used up 'completely' continued to be able to accomplish self-control tasks when they were being told that they would be compensated well for their actions or if their actions would bring benefit to other people. He concluded that having high motivation can overcome weaken self-control.

Will power can also be controlled in the first place to be less vulnerable to being completely depleted. Psychologists often use an analogy to describe will power as being similar to a muscle that will tire out after a lot of exercise. However, there is another element to this analogy. Although muscles will tire due to exercise during the short-term, they become stronger when regularly exercised over the long term. Just like physical exercise, self-control can become stronger when a person exercises willpower.

According to one of the earlier experiments that supports the idea above, the researchers asked participants in the study to follow a two-week guide to improve their moods, track their food intake, or improve their physical posture. Compared to the group that didn't need to exercise self-control, the participants who had to use their willpower by performing willpower heavy exercises were not as vulnerable to the depletion of self-control in a follow-up study.

In another set of research, this researcher found that smokers who exercised willpower for two weeks by avoiding sweet foods or regularly squeezing an exercise handgrip, found more success when it comes to not smoking than other participants who performed two weeks of tasks that didn't require any self-control.

Other researchers have also discovered that using your willpower muscles can help a person increase the strength of their self-control over a period of time. Some researchers in Australia did a study where they assigned participants to a physical exercise program that lasted two months. This is a willpower-required routine. In the conclusion of this program, the participants that finished it scored better when measuring self-control compared to the other participants who were not assigned the exercise program.

The participants that did the program were also reported to have been smoking less, eating healthier food, drinking less alcohol, improving their study habits, and monitoring their spending habits more carefully. Regular exercise of a person's willpower using physical exercise seem to have led to an increase of will power in components of their daily lives.

The research findings regarding how glucose levels are tied to willpower depletion suggest a conceivable solution. A person that maintains their blood sugar by eating regularly and often may be better at helping their brain replenish its storage of willpower. Those who are dieting aim to preserve their willpower while calorie reduction may be more effective by eating frequent and small meals compared to skipping out on entire meals like lunch or dinner.

All this evidence, founded from studies of the depletion of willpower, proposes that people making resolutions for the new year is the worst approach possible. If a person is running low on willpower in one specific area, it often reduces their willpower in all of the other areas. Focusing on one goal at a time makes more sense.

In other words, don't try to get into a healthy diet right away, quit smoking, and start a new workout plan all at the same time. A much better technique is to complete goals one by one. Once you have one single good habit nailed, people no longer need to use their supply of willpower to maintain that behavior. Habits that are healthy will eventually become a part of a person's daily routine and would not need to use the energy of decision-making at all.

There are still many questions regarding the nature of willpower that needs to be answered by future research. However, it seems like if somebody has clear goals, good self-monitoring, and does a little bit of practice, they can train their self-control to be strong when faced with temptation.

## How Self-Discipline Leads to Increased Happiness

A common theme throughout this book is that if you are able to have higher self-discipline and self-control, you will gain more happiness. This has been proven true in numerous different types of research studies. An analysis done on multiple research studies regarding self-discipline found that:

- People who have higher levels of self-discipline feel more happiness in both short-term and long-term.

- People with higher levels of self-discipline are found to have more correlation with social, occupational, and educational success.

- People with the utmost highest levels of self-discipline learn to avoid temptation than to resist every time they are confronted with it.

To some people, practicing self-control may seem like a devil's bargain. This is a trade that allows you to get more things done in the long-term but you have the pay the price of not being able to indulge yourself for personal enjoyment. When we imagine the people who take on this deal, we imagine them as killjoys that get work done, but they never do anything fun. To some people, practicing self-control and discipline seems like a goal that's very far off in the future with little payoff. However, this thought is a huge misconception that can have drastic implications.

There was a study done by professor William Hofmann in 2013 that was published in the Journal of Personality that focused on the relationship between a person's self-control and their happiness. He defined self-control as the ability to change or override a person's inner responses and to interrupt their undesirable behavior tendencies (e.g., our impulses) and prevent ourselves from acting on them.

This study was made up of three experiments that were designed to analyze how a person's happiness was affected by their self-control in the long-term and short-term. The first test had approximately 400 test subjects that read certain statements and decided how well it described them as a person. For instance, the statements would be amongst the lines of "I do certain things that are not good for me, but I will do it if they are fun!" They then filled out a report explaining how happy they were right now and their overall satisfaction with life.

These responses showed a correlation between self-control and a person's life satisfaction, but it also showed that there was a relationship between their self-control and "positive affect". This includes; sentiments, positive emotions, and positive experiences that they have experienced in their day.

In another research study, the participants were asked to carry around smartphones that were programmed to ask them questions at random moments to determine if the person holding it was currently experiencing a desire. If they answered yes, more questions would be asked. These questions focused on how intense the desires were, the details of it, if the person has acted on it or if that desire conflicted with other goals they may have and how much stress the person is feeling due to it.

The results showed that people who had higher self-discipline experienced more positive emotions and less negative emotions.

Researchers decided to investigate this phenomenon even further using a third experiment due to finding that desire-goal conflict causes extra stress to those with low self-discipline.

The third test asked a set of participants to answer questions regarding three regular goal-desired conflicts in their lives. The questions consisted of how severe those conflicts were, how often they occur, and the morality of the choices that were shown to them. After that, they were asked to fill out a survey on their overall life-satisfaction and tendencies related to self-control and self-discipline.

The results surprised all the researchers as they found that people who have higher levels of self-control and discipline had less desire-goal conflicts compared to those with lower self-control and discipline. The conflicts that these high self-control people did face were much less likely to be conflicts regarding choosing a virtuous option. They also discovered that when these conflicts did come up, those with better self-control were more skilled at choosing the better option than the people with lower self-control. This was as expected.

So what does this all mean? All three tests in this series showed that people that have higher levels of self-control were more satisfied in their life, and they felt more positive emotions throughout their daily lives. We can simply stay that using these test results that people who practice and train their self-control generally experience more life satisfaction than the people who don't.

## How Self-Discipline Affects All Aspects of Your Life

As we mentioned earlier in this book, self-discipline affects our personal life, professional life, and our relationships. Without self-discipline, you will simply give yourself up to any gratification that appears before you. For instance, if one of your goals is to bring in more income for your family, self-discipline can help get you there. By achieving this goal, you are improving your personal life, professional life, and likely improving the lives of your family.

Do you see how self-discipline helps you achieve goals and in return, these goals provide a positive impact on other areas of your life? When you are thinking about what goals you want to achieve, aim to set ones that can impact different areas of your life, not just one. For instance, if you are setting a goal to find a significant other to settle down with, it doesn't impact as many areas of your life. It may only impact your relationships, but it does not impact the professional area of your life.

Remember, setting meaningful goals is a huge factor in your success in achieving it. Setting redundant goals such as "I want to finish playing this video game" or "I want to buy myself a new couch" doesn't do much for many aspects of your life. In fact, I wouldn't even classify these goals as goals. They are more so gratifications. This goes without saying to make sure that the goals you are setting are actually goals. Otherwise, you are only lying to yourself, and you are not

actually practicing any self-control or discipline
at all.

# Chapter 5: Failures Are Welcome

An important concept I want you to understand is that failure is welcome when you are practicing self-discipline. Do not begin your journey of increasing self-control thinking that you aren't going to fail. That is only going to discourage you from picking yourself back up. There will be days where you stay in bed instead of going to the gym, or you decide to eat a double cheeseburger instead of choosing a healthier option.

Having failures is completely okay as long as you learn from it and find a way to overcome it next time around. The best way to overcome failure is to prevent it in the first place. If you are going to buy some dinner, don't go to a restaurant that offers unhealthy options. Go to one that ONLY offers healthy options so you have to pick from their selection. If you are planning to go to the gym in the morning, call your workout buddy and ask them to come with you to the gym. That way, you won't want to stand them up so you'll be forced to go.

71

# Edison Mentality

This is where the 'Edison Mentality' comes in. Thomas Edison truly believes that his success was inevitable. He made sure to align all his goals with what his passions were. This created a powerful sense of motivation and optimism that has a positive effect on everyone around him. This included his family, friends, customers, coworkers, investors, and ultimately, the entire nation. He didn't give up the first time he failed on his journey.

He created innovative ways to overcome the obstacles he was faced with. He wasn't disappointed when he faced a problem that halted his progress. He embraced it with open arms because he EXPECTED it. Expect yourself to fail, but create a plan that will help you overcome it. That is how you can use failure to teach yourself more self-discipline.

In fact, permanent failure is usually caused by low self-discipline. That is the failure you don't want. You want to encounter failures that motivate you to grow and increase your self-control and innovative thinking. If you have low self-discipline, even if you promised your workout buddy to meet you at the gym in the morning, you still won't go because you don't value your commitment to the gym and not to your friend.

In order to drop that low self-discipline mindset altogether, let's take a look at some causes of low self-discipline. By understanding what the causes are, you can choose an effective strategy to PREVENT these causes so you can only work towards high self-discipline. Let's take a look.

## Causes of Low Self-Discipline

High self-discipline helps people establish their inner strength and character, enables them to withstand temptation, increases their chance of success, builds better relationships, and has more resistance to feeling offended. We will now discuss some of the causes as to why some people have low self-discipline. Having low self-discipline, not unlike having high self-discipline, affects people's performance in multiple aspects of their life. This includes the performance at work, school, relationships, sports, and financial well-being.

Lack of self-discipline shows up in all the different things that people do in their lives. Some people make sure that they do the big things in life but end up neglecting the little things. They do this to impress other people who don't know them very well. However, they tend to annoy and disappoint those that are close to them because it shows that they don't care enough about the people that they should be showing respect to.

When people choose to not perform certain chores or duties, don't do what they say they would, don't show up for appointments, or don't make themselves presentable for every day, they are showing low self-discipline. So you may be wondering, why don't we take more responsibility for these everyday obligations? Below are two reasons why:

## Reason #1: Bad Attitude

One of the reasons why people don't take more responsibility for everyday obligations is because they don't believe in its importance. Why is this? Why do some people take the time to be considerate, clean, trustworthy, and honest, while others believe that those things are important? The answer is their attitude towards themselves, other people, and life itself. The former believe that people, including themselves, and other forms of life, are worth investing their energy, time, resource, and interest into.

They are able to see the importance of life while the latter have less regard for life and for themselves. All of the simply relates to love. When people have a love for life, they tend to respect all components of it. They take the time to appreciate and experience life as if it's a pleasure. Self-discipline comes from the willingness to take care of ourselves, other people, and other types of life. The lack of discipline shows less willingness to respect themselves or other things.

## Reason #2: Lack of Commitment

The second reason why people don't take more responsibility for everyday obligations is because of the lack of commitment. A person's commitment, enthusiasm, and interest to a task determine the degree to which they can be distracted. When their commitment is very high, very few things have the power to distract them, but if they are doing something that is meaningless to them, their attention is easily distracted.

This proves a strong link between self-discipline and commitment. People who have the inability to ignore, control, or bypass thoughts means that they have low self-discipline. By learning the reasons behind why a person does not take more responsibility for everyday obligations, we are ready to learn the six causes of poor self-discipline.

## Cause #1: Lack of Awareness

The primary cause of low self-discipline is a lack of awareness. This component is important specifically to our imagination and thinking. People are unaware of the thoughts that take our attention are actually negative and can damage a person's well-being.

These thoughts are fed into the conscious mind by the negative mind power to ensure that people have minimal time to spend just simply just being mindful. If people are aware of the things that are happening within their own minds, they would know that self-discipline is needed to refocus our attention away from the flow of negative thoughts.

## Cause #2: Character Weaknesses

People who have weak character often creates poor self-discipline. This includes aspects that have a low level of inner strength, mental toughness, courage, lack of love for other people, an absence of self-love, low interest in self-improvement, apathy, and a version of hard work, shortage of responsibility, lack of self-reflection, high levels of greed, and the inability to ignore temptations in general.

If people place more importance on the desires, thoughts, and emotions that harm them more than the actions, thoughts, and people that help them, it will be difficult for them to develop high self-discipline. Each moment comes with a choice that a person has to make. It can either be something that helps them reach the goals that they have set for themselves, or they can fall into temptation and choose the action that has instant gratification.

## Cause #3: Lack of Ambition

Ambition is very effective in creating self-discipline by giving us a reason to work towards our goals, although we might rather be doing something else. However, it has a negative effect on our self-discipline if our ambition is in an honorable, ethical, or fulfilling one. It is obvious that people who lack the ambition to achieve goals in life will have a harder time building strong self-discipline because they don't have a reason to do it.

This is why we discussed in chapter one that one of the main steps in developing strong self-discipline is coming up with clear and attainable goals. By coming up with a goal that is realistic, an individual can then create a plan of action that they can then hold themselves accountable to. They also need to continue finding the motivation and ambition to keep them striving towards their goals.

## Cause #4: Having Goals That Have Low Importance

People that have goals that aren't that important tend to lack the ambition to achieve them and, therefore, will not be able to practice their self-discipline. If people set goals that looked good on the outside but didn't actually believe that they were necessary, or didn't see them as goals that are important enough to accomplish in the first place, then they may find it very difficult exercise self-discipline in order to put in the work to achieve them.

One of the main motivating factors of self-discipline is having a goal that a person is able to stand by or is important to them. By having an important goal, or something that is meaningful to them, they will be able to find the self-discipline needed in order to complete the tasks required in order to achieve their goal.

## Cause #5: Laziness

There are many temporary reasons as to why a person is not exhibiting self-discipline to do the things that need to be done. This could be sickness, tiredness, apathy, or something that is more appealing that is immediately available. If you find that these excuses are occurring often when you were trying to complete the task needed to reach a goal, you need to dig deep and find the real reason why you are choosing options that aren't the ones that will help you achieve your goal.

Laziness is often the culprit in a lot of cases. The reasons for laziness usually runs very deep into an individual's psyche. If a person believes that there is a goal that is worthwhile, they will be motivated to keep working and applying themselves and making the decisions that make sense when it comes to achieving their goal. However, if they don't have any motivation to achieve their goal, it likely means that their goal isn't important enough, or the person has a natural tendency to be lazy and uninterested.

## Cause #6: Lack of Self-Respect

A person who is lacking self-respect often doesn't put a lot of effort or importance in achieving personal excellence. They often don't really care what others think about them or whether or not they are helping out other people in their lives. You might be wondering what self-respect has to do with self-discipline. The answer is that it takes self-discipline in order to produce excellent results, to achieve goals, and to help people who require it. When a person doesn't think about their own self-improvement, they tend to focus on other things that bring them pleasure such as instant gratification.

They don't necessarily practice self-discipline because they are comfortable in indulging the instant gratification that life throws at them. If a person lacks respect for themselves, they are more likely to indulge in unhealthy conveniences like fast food or shopping impulses that we discussed in chapter one. If a person does have self-respect for themselves, they understand that this instant gratification may bring them joy and pleasure at the moment, but does very little in helping them achieve healthy long-term goals.

By understanding the psychology behind the concept of self-discipline, willpower, and self-control, a person is more likely to see the importance of having these traits if they are a person that wants to achieve the goals they have in life. I strongly believe that everyone has their own personal goals that they want to accomplish in their life.

Those who say they don't may simply be too afraid of failure, and hide their fear behind their lies about how they don't have goals rather than coming to terms with the fact that they are scared of failing to achieve their goals. In the next chapter, we will be discussing why self-discipline is often the key to success. All the concepts and examples that you learned in the past two chapters will slowly come together in chapter 6 you learn why self-discipline is absolutely needed when it comes to a person's ability to find success.

# Chapter 6: The Toolbox

At this point in the book, you should have strong knowledge of what self-discipline is, its benefits, causes of low self-discipline, and how willpower and habits work. You know that a person's willpower is a depletable resource. However, turning your required actions into habits no longer drew from those resources. In this chapter, we will be solidifying your knowledge even more by providing you with tips, guides, and methods to not only help build your self-discipline but to reinforce it as well. We will look at seven tips that help you increase your self-discipline overall. After that, we will look at 10 habits that you need to build in order to train your self-discipline.

## Seven Tips to Help You Reach Your Goal of Self-Discipline

Many researchers suggest that the single most important thing in a person's ability to become successful is their level of self-discipline. Self-discipline is responsible for helping people stay focused on reaching their goals, gives them the grit that they need to stick with difficult tasks, and allows them to overcome barriers and discomforts as they push yourself to achieve greater things.

Rather than trying to be disciplined at everything you do, you can use it to focus on the things that are most important to you. In this chapter, we will be discussing all the reasons why self-discipline is crucial to a person's success. We will be going through multiple reasons as to why this is true, and I will provide you with a few tips that will help increase your self-discipline overall.

1. People cannot achieve their goals without self-discipline.

People cannot achieve their goals without self-discipline, so make sure you are supplementing your goals with a self-discipline list. It will help you focus on the tasks and behaviors that you need to perform in order to achieve the goals that you want. For example, one of my goals is to lose 10 pounds by December. My discipline list will include things like; avoiding fast food, buying more fruits and vegetables, and making sure to hit the gym at least twice a week.

High self-discipline in this example would be doing everything on that list without any exception. This does not mean that you cannot reward yourself or take a break from working towards your goals, it simply means that you should get the things done on your list before you indulge in any rewards.

2. Use a daily "to-do" list to track the things you need to get done

Make sure you are using a daily to-do list to keep track of all the things that you need to get done in order to achieve your goals. Try to use online tools or just a simple notebook that can help you prioritize and organize. It feels very satisfying to be able to check off items that you've completed and it will even motivate you to finish other tasks that are on your list just to feel the satisfaction of being able to check off another box.

Make sure your to-do list works hand-in-hand with your discipline list to help yourself stay on track. A useful tip to keep in mind when you're feeling unmotivated is to start off with the easiest item on the list just to get the ball rolling. Once you complete one easy task people normally feel more motivated than before, this will help you get started on the rest of your list. Starting with a harder task May create apprehension about doing it, therefore, start small and work your way up.

3. <u>Figure out which obstacles are holding you back from success.</u>

Different people have different things that distract them from being able to complete important tasks. For example, a person that is easily distracted by emails and people in their office might have to close their office door as soon as they get into work to get their own tasks done. They may delay any phone calls or meetings unless they're absolutely necessary in order to be able to complete their own set of responsibilities.

This holds true for people that may be trying to lose weight. If they know that junk food is their weakness, instead of having to resist the temptation of eating junk food in their house, they can simply get rid of all the junk food in their house, so they don't have access to it. It is important that you minimize and remove all temptations of the distractions that affect you the most when it comes to reaching your most important goals.

### 4.   Share your goals with other people.

For some people, it may be easier to stick with completing a goal when they have made a public commitment to it. The thought of failing to reach a goal in front of other people can be motivation for the person to stick with it. You can also take this one step further and ask those people to hold you accountable as well. If you aren't sharing your goals with anyone, nobody will know if you have been slacking off from it. When nobody is there to hold you accountable, you will likely be less motivated to keep doing it since nobody will know if you did fail at it.

5. Use external sources or motivation as well as internal.

There is a saying that goes, "don't do it for others, do it for yourself". However, some people find that they are much more disciplined when they know that their impulses, emotions, behaviors, and actions affect other people. Contrary to popular belief, it's alright to use external sources to help your motivation. In fact, sometimes, motivation coming from external sources is more powerful than internal motivation. Find the purpose that's beyond yourself that is important to you in order to help give you a higher chance of success.

6. Discipline is created by creating habits.

We talked about this in the earlier chapter about how when something becomes a habit. You no longer need to draw from your will power bank to get yourself to do it. For example, if a person's goal was to do more exercise, they should make a commitment to work out for at least 20 minutes per day for a whole month. They will be able to see the benefits of regular exercise if they are able to stick with it.

Once they see the benefit, they will have more motivation to keep doing it and soon, it becomes a habit where if this person does not do at least 20 minutes of exercise a day, they don't feel good physically. This way, they will no longer need to draw from their bank of self-control but instead, exercising for them will come naturally since it has become a habit of theirs.

7. <u>Stop making excuses.</u>

Don't procrastinate, or wait for tomorrow, do it now. If you fall off the wagon, that's okay. Start over immediately. Stop telling yourself that something is too hard, or there's something that you cannot change. Don't blame other people for the circumstances that you're in. Making excuses is the Kryptonite of self-discipline. Achieve a mindset that is more about "I can do this" rather than, "I'll do it tomorrow".

# 10 Habits You Need to Build Self-Discipline

How are habits developed and where do they come from? Why is it that when many people try to change their habits by breaking the bad ones or building good ones that they only stick with it for a certain amount of time before they give up and go back to their old ways? The problem here is that the habits that people have had for many years or even decades are the neural pathways that have been imprinted into people's brains.

This happens on a biological level. These neural pathways are responsible for linking up the neural networks in a person's brain to perform a specific function like pouring a cup of coffee in a specific way, walking up the stairs, or smoking a cigarette.

These neural pathways are responsible for the automation behavior that is constantly used in an effort to reduce the energy needed for the conscious processing power in a person's brain. By doing this, it allows a person's mind to focus on other things rather than the habitual tasks that they have done a thousand times. This function came from our early human days and is actually a part of our DNA. It allows humans to have a mind that is more efficient so it can be used to do other things rather than always being used to do mundane things.

In this case, it's usually the mundane behaviors that people repeat most often which hold them back from building good habits. People have the tendency to build more bad habits that bring negativity to their lives rather than building more good habits that aid them in achieving their goals further. Since the cause of this is the ingrained neural pathways, it is difficult for people to give up bad habits or form new and good ones when the bad ones are constantly getting in the way.

However, if you can try to ingrain the next following habits we will be discussing into your life, you will find that strengthening your self-discipline may become easier. Again, these things don't happen overnight. Habits take time to build and form. By starting small and building, you will stop thinking about how much longer you can discipline yourself since you will have ingrained those habits into your brain, which then automatically promotes the self-discipline that you seek.

## Habit #1: Gratitude

Gratitude is an important action in human life that helps not only people with self-discipline but is often used to help people that are facing self-esteem and self-confidence issues. A huge problem in our modern world today is that we are constantly presented with millions of materialistic things that cause us to always be wanting something more or something else.

This causes people to spend too much time thinking about all the things that they want, and not enough time thinking about the things that they already have. Building gratitude can help people to stop wanting the things that they don't have and move forward towards appreciating the things that they do have. When people do this, they can begin to make remarkable changes in their lives.

The effects of practicing and showcasing gratitude are extremely crucial. It does everything from improving mental health, emotional well-being, a person's spirituality, gratitude is capable of so many things. Practicing gratitude is an exercise that is constantly used in therapy to help the client move away from thinking about things that aren't in the present and focus on being mindful.

Ultimately, gratitude helps people move away towards a state of abundance and away from a state of lack. When people live in a state of lack, it makes it impossible for them to focus on achieving their goals and being self-disciplined. They spend too much of their mental energy and capacity worrying about the things that they don't have or living in a fearful way, to the point that they forget about the things that they do have.

The state of lack can also show up in someone as physical symptoms. This state produces a lot of stress because the brain automatically releases cortisol and epinephrine which are the stress hormones from our brains. These hormones impact numerous systems within the human body. When someone is stressed, their immune systems, digestive systems, and reproductive systems are all affected.

We must spend some time every day writing down everything we are grateful for. Even if you feel like there's nothing you are grateful for, dig deep to identify one thing. It doesn't have to be anything large, like winning the lottery or finding $20 on the ground. It could be something very simple like the nice weather, the nice conversation that you had with your barista, or even just seeing a cute dog on your way home.

## Habit #2: Forgiveness

If you are someone living a fast-paced life, how often do you find yourself feeling angry, frustrated, or annoyed? Due to the insane amount of convenience we are offered in our daily lives, simple annoyances that happen in a person's day can cause a spiral of negative emotions.

For example, if you are in a hurry to get to work and you happen to be running late that day, the coffee shop that you normally stop at to get your morning coffee is taking forever to make your order. When you finally get your coffee, you realize that they had made your order wrong but now you have no time to get it fixed. That one simple human error has spent you into a spiral of anger and annoyance, and you struggle to let go of it and you find that it is still negatively impacting your whole day.

This causes you to have spent most of your energy upset about the coffee shop that wronged you, and you don't have enough mental capacity to focus on other things like practicing your self-discipline. When people spend most of their days feeling the emotions of anger, regret, or guilt, they actually are creating more problems than they are with solutions. The emotions of anger and hate consume much more energy in a person's body compared to positive emotions like forgiveness and love. Forgiveness is something that can be learned.

Without learning forgiveness, people would simply not be able to achieve self-discipline. When a person is too worried about how someone or something has wronged them, it makes it impossible for them to focus on achieving their goals or on their personal discipline. If someone has hurt you in the past, try to learn forgiveness to forgive them. This doesn't necessarily mean that you have to forget about what they did to you altogether.

Simply just forgive and let go of that negative energy and give it back to the universe rather than keeping it within your body. When we perform the act of forgiveness, we are actually letting go of the negative energy that inhibits our ability to practice self-discipline.

To master self-discipline, you have to get rid of sources that are sucking away at your mental energy. Holding on to negative emotions like anger is a sure way for your energy to be drained. While forgiveness might not seem like a discipline habit when you first look at it, it is an extremely crucial one to build in the process.

Try to think about something that you are currently angry with. It could be someone that you think has wronged you recently, or simply just an annoying situation that has happened to you. Instead of just thinking about how it made you feel, try to put yourself in their shoes. What would be the things that you would do if you were in their situation? Make it light-hearted and try to find some humor in it. Rather than thinking about it as a situation that shouldn't have happened, try to find a lesson learned in those situations. I know that it is very hard to forgive certain people, especially if they have really hurt you or wronged you in life.

However, it isn't until people are able to give up their hurt before things in their life really began to improve. People are often too busy stressing and worrying that they don't spend enough time thinking about how they are going to change their future.

## Habit #3: Meditation

Just like gratitude, meditation is a commonly used technique to help people practice mindfulness in cases where they are suffering from an anxiety disorder or depression disorder. Meditation is something that can be used to help put people's minds at ease. When people meditate, they take their awareness away from things of the past and the future and focus it on the things of the present. When this happens, they are able to connect themselves to the universe, which also helps them with increasing gratitude.

In the next chapter, we will learn the specific ways of how meditation can help a person improve their self-discipline. Meditation actually plays a big role in a person's ability to use their willpower. Its function is to clear the mind of any thoughts and simply focus all attention on the present. From a self-discipline perspective, meditation helps set the right tone for a person's day. In addition, it helps people improve their physical, emotional, and mental health whilst allowing them to gain numerous benefits for the least amount of time invested.

There are many types of meditation, some of which focuses on mindfulness and some of which focus on love and gratitude. There truly are too many different types of meditation for humankind to keep track of, but the most popular and beneficial type that is used amongst many therapies and within self-discipline is mindfulness meditation. Contrary to common belief, meditation doesn't require a lot of time. It can be done in less than 15 minutes.

However, the hardest part of meditation is actually bringing yourself to do it. A person has to be able to keep their mind still and train it to stop wandering all the time. The trick behind mindfulness meditation is not to stop wandering thoughts altogether, but simply to acknowledge these thoughts and reroute yourself back to the present. There are many types of breathing techniques that can be accompanied with meditation to help with achieving mindfulness.

We will be diving deeper into these techniques in the next chapter.

Some people believe that meditation is about aligning the physical human body with its spiritual body. However, for the purpose of this book, we will stay away from spirituality and focus more on the practical benefit that being mindful can bring.

## Habit #4: Active Goal Setting

We have mentioned this briefly in the previous chapter, but it is important enough that we will mention it again. We learned in the previous chapter that setting attainable goals is more effective than setting Broad and large goals. by setting smaller goals, it becomes something that is more quantifiable, and because of this, you can easily keep track of how you are doing when it comes to goal achievement.

Active goal setting differs greatly from passive goal-setting. Passive goal setting means you are setting goals within your head, and they are passive because they don't have enough details.

102

Passive goal-setting means that a person hasn't properly defined the actual goal which makes it hard for them to keep track of their progress and knowing what needs to be done in order to achieve that goal.

Active goal setting is the complete opposite of passive goal-setting. Active goal setting means writing out these goals and making sure that they have an important meeting. These goals have to be measurable and very specific. To successfully have an active goal, a person has to make a plan towards achieving it. this is why people set long-term goals, but also engage in smaller goals on a daily basis in order to work towards achieving the bigger goal.

By using active goal-setting, it ingrains the discipline in us because you are forced to give it direction. By breaking down your big goals into smaller daily goals, it helps people avoid distractions by only looking at the things that they need to get done in the present day. This way, a person isn't left constantly thinking about one large intimidating goal but not knowing how to approach it.

Active goal setting works by taking the first step in setting your long-term goals. If you are someone that has long-term goals like; wanting to own your first home, wanting to pay off your student debt by the next three years, or wanting to take 6 months off to travel Europe. If you are someone that has long-term goals, then you need to actively participate in daily, weekly, and monthly goal setting and planning. You have to play an active role in tracking your progress towards your goals and making changes in places where you feel like aren't working for you.

So take out a pen and a piece of paper and start writing down what long-term goals you have. Once you have some long-term goals written down, break it down into monthly, weekly, and daily goals. Start slowly by accomplishing your daily goals and when you reach the end of the month, assess to see if you have achieved your monthly goal through accomplishing your daily goals. If you haven't, look back on your daily goals and see if there's anything you can change so that you could achieve next month's goal.

## Habit #5: Eat Healthy

We also discussed the benefits of eating healthy in the previous chapter but we will expand on it a little bit more here. What a lot of people don't realize is that our human body spends a huge portion of its energy digesting and processing food. When a person's diet is rich in proteins, fats, and carbohydrates, their body is actually using more energy to process food, which some of it is useless to us.

Raw fruits and foods actually offer the biggest boost of energy for humans because they require less energy for the body to process and provides more energy for the body to use after that. This process is called an enhanced Thermic Effect of Food (TEF) or otherwise known as Dietary Induced Thermogenesis (DIT).

Like we learned in the previous chapter, our brains use up a large amount of glucose in order to keep it functioning. Therefore, the amount of energy that a person has is very responsible and how focused they feel. When a person is focused, they can achieve their goals using less willpower than if they weren't focused. When a person is feeling too comatose from the unhealthy food that they have eaten, staying focused is something that is very hard to achieve. They often spend too much of their time feeling too sluggish and tired to work on achieving their goals.

You commonly hear that breakfast is the most important meal of the day. However, eating multiple healthy meals throughout the day should be your priority. In order to do this, you have to actively plan what you're going to eat during these meals in order to break some of your bad habits. For example, if you are planning to eat five healthy smaller-sized meals per day, but you haven't prepared any of those meals, you are more likely to feel hungry and indulge in unhealthy conveniences like fast food.

If you are someone that eats fast food or processed foods often, your body won't be able to create enough energy to help you approach your goals with focus or help you have the willpower in order to start working at them.

Since the food that a person eats can change the neural chemical makeup of their brain, it also heavily influences a person's mind and body connection. Take a look at the things that you eat during your day. Try to find the meals where you often indulge in unhealthy food or junk food. Plan in advance so you can substitute those meals with raw, organic, and healthy foods. By buying this type of healthy food in advance and preparing it for the times that you become hungry, you will be less likely to visit your nearest McDonalds.

## Habit #6: Sleep

Since the theory behind willpower is that it gets its energy from the brain, which gets its energy from glucose levels and rest, then it's safe to assume that sleep is directly connected to how the brain is able to acquire energy. When a person doesn't get enough sleep, their brain spends most of its energy focused on just keeping your basic body functions up and going.

This does not leave much energy for a person to spend on exerting their willpower, practicing self-discipline, or even simply just remembering their self-discipline. Getting a healthy amount of sleep is a crucial requirement for accomplishing anything. When a person doesn't get enough sleep, it affects their ability to focus, their judgment, their mood, their overall health, and their diet.

When people suffer chronic sleep deprivation such as insomnia, things go from bad to worse. Many research studies have found evidence that people who don't get a healthy amount of sleep regularly have a greater risk of catching specific diseases. People who don't sleep enough can have their immune system negatively impacted. This can cause a person to frequently catch colds or flu that cause them to not have the ability to go to school, work, or get anything effective done.

For an adult, it is important to get at least six hours of sleep every night. A healthy amount of sleep should range between eight to ten hours every night, but the minimum amount is 6 hours. Avoid eating or drinking anything that contains caffeine at least 5 hours before your bedtime so that it doesn't affect your natural sleep cycle. Make a note to also stay away from ingesting too many toxins during the day such as cigarettes, alcohol, drugs, or prescription medicine if it can be avoided.

In conclusion, the benefits of getting enough sleep are extraordinary. Aside from the fact that it can help you stay focused and be more disciplined, it also helps you curb inflammation and pain, lower stress, improves your memory, jumpstarts your creativity, sharpens your attention, improves your grades, limits your chances for accidents and helps you avoid depression.

## Habit #7: Exercise

Exercise is one of the most important habits to build within all people. It acts as a cornerstone habit to help a person's life be filled with positive habits and be rid of the bad ones. A person that is truly able to discipline themselves has to instill the habit of exercise into their everyday routine. As you all may already know, there are endless benefits when it comes to exercise. This is something that is talked about not only by psychologists but medical experts as well. Even though exercise is such an important component of a person's life, not everyone actually makes it a priority. Why is this?

In our busy modern-day lives, everyone is caught up with trying to get all the things that they need to get done and are often busy running around completing errands and fail to simply tackle exercise head-on. Often, people have a bad mindset when it comes to exercise and think that they won't be able to build it as a habit because they simply have "too many other things to do". This is where most people are wrong. There are ways to incorporate exercise even if their day is jam-packed from beginning to end.

When people think of exercise, they may automatically think of a minimum one-hour intense weight-lifting session at the gym, a one-hour long, expensive spin class, or a one-hour yoga class. If that's what they are thinking about then yes, it is true that the people that have busy lives may not be able to incorporate the time to get to their exercise class, the time it takes to complete the exercise class, and then get to wherever they need to go after that.

However, exercise doesn't necessarily have to be a formalized session that takes a long time. It can simply be getting some sit-ups, push-ups, or some jumping jacks in the morning before you head to work. It can also be you choosing to walk to work instead of taking the bus, or it could be a brief walk around your neighborhood park after dinner.

By instilling exercise as a keystone habit of your life, it can help you become more disciplined and can also improve your life in numerous ways. First of all, exercise is extremely effective in reducing stress levels and pain because it causes the brain to release feel-good endorphins and neurotransmitters like serotonin and dopamine. Secondly, exercise helps increase the oxygenation and blood flow of body cells which is responsible for helping boost the immune system and fighting off diseases. Lastly, exercise increases a person's ability to focus on the task at hand due to the increased activity in the brain which allows us to live a more disciplined life.

So start building the habit of exercise in your life by simply just going for a 10-minute walk or just doing some sit-ups and push-ups right after you wake up. Just a few minutes is fine. Try to do this for one week and then increase the amount of time you spend on that session for the next week. Keep up with this pattern and soon enough, you will have a healthy amount of time every day that you set aside to get your exercise in, and this is when it will become a full-blown habit.

## Habit #8: Organization

Have you ever noticed that when your home is messy, it makes it very hard to be comfortable and therefore leads you to be unfocused and distracted? Naturally, humans don't like living in a dirty and messy environment. In order for a person to achieve their goals and accomplish self-discipline, they need to be organized. Organization also needs to become a habit that is fully incorporated in a person's personal life and professional life. This includes the physical act of organizing the things you have in your home and the mental act of organizing the things on your mind.

By living an organized life, you are living a disciplined life. If you are someone, who is constantly scattered and disorganized, start small with your organization skills. Just pick one small space each day for yourself to organize. This can be just one single drawer in your kitchen, the things lying around on your desk, or just straighten out the things on your coffee table. The next day, pick something else to organize like your bathroom drawers or the clothes in your closet.

The more time you spend living in a clean and organized environment, the less you would want your home to become cluttered and messy again. You will start to begin to notice when clutter builds up and by having a habit of organization, you will immediately organize things as you use them, so you don't have to spend time organizing it later on.

By decluttering your home or your working environment, you will have plenty of different areas where you can sit down and work on your own goals. Has your home ever been so cluttered that when you do have the motivation to start working on something, you simply just don't have the space to do it? In order to avoid this, keep your home clean and organized at all times so that when you have a rush of motivation, you can find a workspace that is clean and ready for you to work.

Like a lot of other habits, the habit of organization can be learned and built over time. It does require your attention and effort but it is something that will pay off tremendously in the long run. When you are living in a physical space that is organized and clean, your mind will automatically become more stress-free, relaxed, and give you the ability to focus.

In turn, by becoming more organized, you are increasing your ability to be more self-disciplined. Begin to incorporate this good habit of putting things back where it belongs when you're finished using it rather than leaving it out. Little things like this we do on a daily basis have the largest impact on the quality of life. Pay attention to small things, and you'll begin to see big benefits.

## Habit #9: Time Management

In the busy world that we live in today, time management is extremely crucial if you are trying to get everything that you need to get done. An average person has to work 40 hours a week, not including the time it takes for them to commute to work, and still have to make time for things like exercise, relationships, socializing, family, and achieving the goals that they have set. Without good time management, it will be virtually impossible for anyone to get anything done unless they are able to manage their time effectively.

When people are able to properly manage their time, they will begin to have room to do the things that actually matter. Mainly, they must make room to do the activities that they need in order to achieve the goals that they have set. In order for a person to achieve their long-term goals, they have to break it down into smaller daily goals that may not be the most urgent but are definitely still very important. If a person does not have good time management, they likely cannot even get the most urgent things that they need to get done in a day, let alone achieving goals that don't require immediate urgency.

To effectively measure if certain things are urgent, non-urgent, important, not important, you need to take a second to think about whether or not the action that you are doing is not 'urgent but important' or 'not urgent and not important' or 'urgent and important'. The things that fall into the 'not urgent and not important' category are known as things that are time-wasters. This includes things like browsing social media on your phone or binge-watching your favorite Netflix series.

Things that fall into the category of 'not urgent but important' are likely the short-term goals you have set for yourself. Although they don't need to be urgently completed, they are still important for your self-growth. Things that are urgent and important are likely deadlines or any responsibilities that you have to complete for your work.

A person's ability to strengthen self-discipline is derived from their ability to manage their time. Some of the most successful people in the world are incredible time managers because rather than using time as a detractor, they use time as a benefit. Everybody has the same amount of time in a day. We shouldn't waste it.

Start managing your time by categorizing the things you need to do in a day with the categories I gave you above. Start by doing the things that are both urgent and important then move on to the things that are not urgent but important. Leave the things that are both not urgent or important to the end of the day when you have completed all the other things. This way, you are maximizing your time to get the things that you need to get completed.

## Habit #10: Persistence

This last habit you probably saw coming. No amount of self-discipline would ever be complete without the presence of persistence. Persistence is a type of habit that helps us to not give up even when we are faced with failure. Persistence is what helps us get back up on our feet to keep trying even when we do fail. Persistence plays such a huge role in self-discipline that without it, achieving self-discipline is probably impossible.

You might be wondering why that is. This is because achieving our goals is not an easy thing to do. It is really hard. Getting discouraged is easy and something that happens to everyone along their journey. In addition, giving up takes far less energy and effort compared to continuing to push through even if it's something that causes a lot of pain in the process before it can give us any pleasure.

However, this hardship that is required to achieve any goals is simply something that you have to persevere through because that's just what it takes. We all have to realize that even the most successful people in the world have failed numerous times over and over again. Failure is simply a part of life, and rather than avoiding it and not pursuing your goals at all in fear of failure, we should learn to persevere and push through even during the hardest of times. Without fail, we wouldn't be able to achieve the big goals that we have set for ourselves.

There are many ways that a person can go about instilling perseverance as a habit, but the best and most effective weight is to come up with the reasons why you want to do the things in life that you aim for. If the reasons behind your goals are strong enough, they can motivate you so you can get through anything.

Photo by Sage Friedman on Unsplash

# Chapter 7: Visualization and Meditation for Personal Growth

In this chapter, we will learn two methods that will help you achieve your goals and to strengthen your self-discipline at the same time. I will teach you about visualization and how using it can improve your performance in virtually anything. After that, we will learn about how we can use meditation and mindfulness to achieve your goals.

## The Visualization Method – Using It to Achieve Your Goals

Most people have tried to visualize their goals at least a couple of times in their lives. They probably spend a lot of time visualizing a desired future event. For the general public, visualization is a process where they picture their future within their minds. However, visualization can be used for much more than just that. It is a type of inner transformation that leads to seeing actual results in reality.

Visualization is also a form of creative thinking where a person can shape their life using a specific purpose within their mind. The best part about the image is that a person may have envisioned is that it doesn't have to rely upon the external events of the outer world. It can depend entirely on a person's imagination.

Within a person's inner world, they can be anyone or anything that they choose to be. It doesn't matter what is happening externally, as it doesn't make a difference to the conscious process of visualization. You might be thinking that this sounds very airy-fairy. Don't be under the wrong assumption here. Visualization isn't just 'fantasizing'. It is both a proactive and conscious activity where a person is able to actively visualize things or events in their mind in a specific and certain order to help them positively impact their reality.

Therefore, visualization has a strong connection to the actual world that you live in, but it is not

100% dependent on it. Visualization argues that how a person behaves within the outer world of reality is dependent on how the person creates their internal world for themselves every day.

## Visualization is the Key to Improved Performance

Here is something that not many people know: Visualizing an action or a skill before actually performing it is nearly as powerful as physically performing that action in reality. Scientific studies have found evidence that people's thoughts actually produce the same instructions in their mind as it does with actions. This means that when somebody is mentally rehearsing or practicing something in their mind using the visualization process, it actually impacts the many cognitive processes within a person's brain that includes planning, motor control, memory, and attention perception.

In layman's terms, the way a person's brain is stimulated when they are visualizing an action is exactly the same as when they are actually performing it physically. Therefore, scientists can safely assume that the act of visualization provides just as much value as physically performing a task.

Many athletes in certain sports use the act of visualization to help themselves train before a competition. For example, in Olympic cycling, the cyclist will prepare for a competition by closing their eyes and visualizing the racetrack in their mind. They move their bodies while visualizing the way that they will travel through the racetrack in order to train their muscle memory and reflexes even further.

This way, when they do begin to compete on the racetrack, they have already visualized themselves cycling through it using the strategies that they have been taught and visualized in their minds. This is a technique and training skill that many professional coaches teach their athletes to do.

When a person is visualizing, their conscious mind is aware that what they're visualizing is not real but is just a result of imagination.

Consequently, a person's subconscious isn't able to differentiate the difference between what a person is thinking and what they are actually doing. In other words, a person's inner-mind isn't able to distinguish the difference between real life, a photo, past memories, or an imagined future.

Rather, the mind is under the impression that everything a person sees is real. This is proven by numerous brain scans that scientists have conducted over the years, where they discovered that there are no brain activity differences when someone is observing something in the real world compared to when a person is visualizing.

All of this evidence is extremely important because it points the theory that visualization can help people learn new skills and be able to reprogram and rewire their brains without having to perform physical actions. For example, if somebody is looking to increase their self-esteem, they can use the process of visualization by imagining themselves doing those actions before actually doing it in the real world.

Just like how this method is effective for a person to increase their self-esteem, this is also very helpful for people that are looking to increase their self-discipline because it helps minimize the feelings of anxiety. By using the technique of working through scenarios in a person's mind can help them effectively require their brain in order to build new patterns, habits and behaviors, which makes completing tasks in the real world far less anxiety-ridden. Due to this, bringing your visualizations to life will help you feel more at ease.

## How Worries Are Reprogramming Your Brain

When a person is experiencing negative emotions like anxiety, fear, worry, or stress, they are performing negative visualization. This is a type of visualization that happens unconsciously, where the person is not aware that they are negatively visualizing, but it is still a type of visualizing nonetheless.

Every time a person stresses or worries about something, they often suffer from having anxiety or fear about what they think may happen in the future. They are actually in a moment of visualizing negative events. In addition, in that moment, the person is actually rewiring their own brain in limiting ways. Just like how a person's brain can be reprogrammed and rewire to build/improve positive and helpful habits, it is also possible that it can be rewired negatively.

***If you are interested in gaining a better understanding of anxiety disorders, I wrote a book on the subject that you can find on Amazon. Go to the last page of this book and you will find the direct link.***

Every time a person indulges in the worries that they're in at the moment, they are building on the existing neural pathways within their brain. Due to this, every time a person envisions something negative, it causes negative worries much easier. When a person is visualizing negative events, it can make a person feel uneasy or anxious at that moment. A person's subconscious mind can't actually distinguish the difference between what it actually sees and a visualization.

Due to this, the person's brain processes those events as if it's a physical action that you have performed. This results in the neural networks forming in their brain which creates new beliefs, habits, and perspectives. Ultimately, the person is effectively building new patterns by rewiring their brain to support all the things that they have negatively envisioned.

When a person does that, they are building patterns of behavior and skills that aren't helpful. The more frequently a person thinks about this pattern, the easier it is for their mind to keep replaying that pattern repeatedly until the action of worrying becomes a habit that is triggered when a person faces any level of uncertainty. In addition to this, when a person worries about certain things, those things have a higher chance of manifesting within their life.

This happens because when a person focuses on negative things, they are doing it using the **Reticular Activating System**. This person's brain is searching for anything it could around them that would support those worries. Due to this, everything a person sees will then validate all the things that they worry about. In addition, every time a person makes bad decisions or choices based on their flawed perspective, it leads to them have their worries manifested into their real world.

This all sounds very incredible, I know. The best part about this is that the exact process that is at play when someone is visualizing negative things also works in a positive way with the goals that they want to achieve. This process initiates the Reticular Activating System and supports people to have more awareness of the events, opportunities, and other people that are related to their goals.

This leads to the person making conscious and subconscious choices based on that information, which helps them achieve their goals in reality.

Due to this, you can use visualization in an empowering and helpful way. However, keep in mind that it can also be used in a negative and unhelpful way. Whichever one you choose is a choice you can make.

## Positive Visualization Techniques

In this subchapter, we will be taking a look at four different types of visualization techniques that a person can use to help improve their life. These techniques include:

- Mastering a new skill.

- Healing your mind and body.

- Achieving your goals.

- Creating an action plan.

We will be learning about the process of the steps that a person can follow in each of those areas while also discussing the benefits of those techniques. Let's dive right in.

## Mastering a New Skill

Visualization can be used to not only learn a new skill but to master it as well. Visualization is really effective in mastering new skills because due to how the brain is exactly the same when stimulated. Someone who is visualizing the skill has the same brain activity as when they physically do that skill. Let's take a look at a study that an Australian psychologist did that studied the effectiveness of visualization regarding a person's ability to do free throws in basketball.

This psychologist chose three groups of students at random who have never tried visualization before. The first group practiced the skill of free throwing for 20 days straight. The second group only practiced free throws twice, once on the very first day and once on the last day. The third group did the same. However, the third group spent half an hour every day visualizing themselves practicing free throws. If they had "missed" in their visualized free throw, they "practiced" getting it right the next time.

On the last day of this study, the psychologists measured how the participants improved using percentages. The group that got physical practice every day improved their free throws by 24%. The second group that only practiced twice did not improve at all. However, the third group who had practiced just as much as the second group did 23% better, nearly the same as the first group.

At the end of this experiment, the psychologist published a paper that was about how most effective visualization happens when the visualizer is able to see what they are doing. In other words, the ones that practiced visualizing the free-throw actually 'felt' the basketball in their hands and 'saw' it go through the hoop and have heard it 'bounce'.

You can also use visualization to improve upon any skills you want to learn. Make sure that you try to utilize all your senses when you are visualizing yourself do this. Below are a **simple 5 steps** to how you can use visualization to do this:

1.  Choose a skill that you are interested in mastering.

2.  Identify what your real-world proficiency level is in this skill.

3.  Visualize yourself doing this skill in as much detail as you can using all five senses.

4.  Repeat this visualization for 11 days at 20 minutes per day.

5.  Perform this skill physically and keep track of measuring your improvement. Continue visualizing while doing that skill in real life if you are not satisfied with the results.

### *Creating an Action Plan*

If you are feeling overwhelmed or stressed, creating a plan of action using visualization can help you relax and motivate you to take action. This technique is most effective if you use it before you go to bed so you can start planning the next day's work. However, you can use this technique throughout the day if you have 10 minutes of free time.

Below are three simple steps on how to do this:

1. Calm yourself down, and make sure you are feeling relaxed. Sit down as it will help you get some rest from whatever you were doing before.

2. Close your eyes and start to visualize which things specifically that you want to accomplish for tomorrow. Now, visualize those actions that you'd like to do in as much detail as you can and then ask yourself these questions below:

   a. How do I want to feel?

   b. How will I interact with others?

   c. What specific actions do I want to take?

   d. What do I want?

   e. What obstacles will I potentially face?

   f. How will I overcome obstacles?

   g. What do I want to achieve?

3. The reality here is that people are not able to predict all the things that might happen to them. When events happen unexpectedly, they can often ruin any plans that have been put in place. However, good planning isn't about planning around all possible obstacles, but it is more about adapting to the obstacles that life gives you. When you keep this in mind, it is important that you affirm with yourself at the end of your session with "this or something better will come my way". By giving yourself affirmation, you are keeping your mind open to endless possibilities. This will result in you be more ready and okay with making adjustments when unexpected things happen to you.

This process is definitely not a foolproof plan. However, this visualization will help you with envisioning possible situations that might happen. These scenarios will allow you to be able to make better decisions as you continue to work towards your goals.

## Achieving Your Goals

This visualization technique is the most important one when it comes to strengthening self-discipline. By using the technique of visualization for setting goals brings a lot of value but this technique does come with one major drawback. The most popular form of visualization is goal setting. Most people have definitely used visualization pertaining to their goals at one time or another. However, this technique may not have worked for them due to one critical flaw.

This flaw is that when people are visualizing their goals, they only focus on visualizing their end goal and nothing in between. They see within their mind's a big and flashy awesome goal that's going to be rainbows and butterflies. Yes, they are experiencing this using all of their sensory but they simply open their eyes after the visualization feeling very inspired. However, this type of motivation is extremely short-lived because the next time this person faces an obstacle, it immediately deflates their motivation.

When this happens, people feel the need to visualize their goal again in order to create more motivation. However, because nothing happens every time they visualize their goal, their motivation doesn't grow either. In fact, every time a person hits an obstacle and they try the process of visualization again, their motivation becomes weaker every time, and they start to lose more and more energy.

The mistake that these people are making is that they are nor properly visualizing their goals. They are only seeing the destination, but they don't understand that achieving a goal takes much more than just that. Achieving a goal is part of a journey that is full of emotional highs and lows, wins and losses, and a journey of ups and downs. Due to this, these are the things that a person would also need to include in their visualization.

When a person visualizes their end goal, it is very effective in creating that desire and hunger.

However, the proper way to use visualization is to only spend 10 percent of your time visualizing the end goal and spending the rest of the visualization time thinking about HOW you will achieve your goals and overcome challenges. In some ways, it's similar to the form of visualization planning that we just discussed.

A person's end goal helps keep inspiration running in the long term, but it is the journey that helps a person stay motivated in the short term. The way to maximize the time spent on achieving small goals to get to your end goal, you must visualize those as well.

Below are **five steps** that you can follow to achieve this visualization:

1. Get yourself to a quiet place and sit down and close your eyes. Start to visualize your end goal. Imagine yourself experiencing and living this goal using all five of your senses.

2. Slowly take a few steps backward from your end goal and start to visualize the process

that you took that lead to you achieving your end goal. Imagine all the problems and you faced that put you back. However, you can see yourself finding solutions to those problems. Continue visualizing until you are all the way back to the present moment.

3. Now, move forward with time and visualize how you took on opportunities that helped you overcome your problems.

4. At the end of this visualization, take a few moments to send your future self some positive energy for their journey.

5. When you exit the visualization, emotionally detach from the outcome of your goal. The thing that can hold you back is if you are having an emotional attachment to a specific result. Instead, try to stay open-minded and be flexible for what's to come on your journey.

You can use visualization using those steps on a daily or weekly basis. Weekly sessions can be as long as 30 minutes and you can keep your daily sessions shorter, so they are between 5 - 10 minutes. However, be sure that you are using your daily sessions to visualize the next steps of achieving your goal for the upcoming week. This will help you continue moving forward to reach your goal. After that, you can use your weekly visualizations using the five steps above.

## Using Meditation to Achieve Your Goals

One of the most powerful and inspiring things that humans can do is being able to visualize the things that they want to manifest and then actually making it happen. The power of the human mind is extraordinary, especially when it is coupled with mindfulness practices like meditation. Using meditation, a person can increase their ability and make heaps of progress towards the life that they want to create for themselves.

Goal setting is the first action that a person needs to make in order to reach their goals. The purpose behind setting a goal is so that a person would be able to achieve their desired results. When a goal is set carefully with focus, momentum, action, and intention, setting and achieving goals is the first step a person needs to take in order to move from where they are not to where they want to be. However, they need to know where it is that they want to be. The "where" begins with a person envisioning it.

The first step to this is to start with imaging the end in mind and work backward (this is what we discussed earlier in this chapter). Many people mistake their goal for vision, thinking when the goal is actually the end result. They will set a goal without thinking about what the goal will allow them to do, be, or have in the long term. In order for a person to make the most out of their goal-setting process, it is important to think about what quality of lifestyle they would want to ultimately achieve. For the purpose of clarity, let's talk a little bit more between a person's vision and their goal.

### *Your Vision vs. Your Goal*

A person's vision isn't something that needs to be created from scratch; in fact, it is something that already exists inside them. They simply need to get in touch with it. A person's vision is the big picture of their desired outcomes. It represents the most important things to that person and is often compelling, inspiring, exciting, and filled with many positive emotions.

A goal, on the other hand, is different. A goal is very specifically designed that requires tasks that need to be completed in order to get to the thing that they want at the end of their journey. The downside here is that a person's goal may not initiate those positive emotions that become an inspiration. Goals act more like stepping stones on a path that will lead you to your ultimate end goal.

The most popular and effective way to build your goals is using the SMART goals format. You may have done or heard of this before at your workplace or while you were in school. SMART stands for specific, measurable, achievable, resources, and time. This helps you make sure that your goals are specific and concise, you have a way of measuring them, they are goals that are achievable, you have or have a way of getting the necessary resources, and you have a timeline in which you want your goals to be met.

By using imagery that is vivid and highly detailed, it is a very powerful way for someone to train their mind to go after the things that they want. Remember when we discussed how athletes often use visualization to help themselves train? For example, famous golf athlete Tiger Woods has been using visualization to help train his golfing techniques ever since he was a teenager.

Even the NBA star Michael Jordan used mental imagery to help get himself into the mindset that he wants to be in order to make his famous three-point shots. If professional athletes use visualization techniques, they can enhance their ability to be the best. You can also use visualization and meditation to help you achieve your goals.

### *10 Steps to Meditation to Help You Achieve Your Goals*

In this ten-step guide, we will be using a mix of visualization and meditation to guide you into focusing on your goals. This is very similar to what we learned with visualization, researchers have found that by visualizing and meditating to the process of a person achieving their goals, i will help them to actually do it in real life. Try these following steps of guided meditation to help put your goal into the future:

1. Start by thinking of an area of your life in your mind. Choose something where you have been struggling with, or you would like to change.

2. Now start to imagine the best possible outcome that you would like to be living in regards to the area that you've selected Imagine this 6 to 12 months from now What is the reality that you are looking to

achieve? Try not to get caught up with any negativity or limitations; instead, just allow yourself to imagine and get carried away with your strongest goals.

3. Focus your mind on connecting with just one goal that you would like to achieve over the next three months. Make sure your goal is a good one and is as meaningful as possible. If you choose a goal that isn't meaningful or doesn't hold a lot of weight, the end result won't feel special for you. Make sure to choose something that is significant enough so that once you achieve this goal, you will feel a high sense of accomplishment and motivation for your next goal. Be sure to run your goal through the SMART acronym to ensure that it is a goal that is set up for success.

4. Now that you are starting to feel connected with the goal that you've set, try to imagine what your life will be like once you achieve the goal. Visualize a

picture or movie in your mind and try to view it as if you are looking at it through your own pair of eyes. Factor in all the other sensory perceptions to try to imagine the most real and positive feelings. Where are you? Who is with you? What are the things happening around you?

5. Now, begin to step out of the picture or movie that you've imagined and begin to imagine yourself floating up in the air above where you are sitting now while taking that imagery with you. Take a deep breath and as you breathe out, use your breath to give life to the image and fill it with intention and positive energy. Repeat this five times.

6. In this step, it is time to imagine yourself floating out into the future while imagining yourself dropping the imagery that you've created for your goal down into your real-life below you at the exact

time and date that you've set for yourself to reach this goal.

7. Pay attention to all the things that need to happen between then and now and how it is beginning to re-evaluate itself in order to support you in achieving that goal. Visualize this process and all those events to make it feel as realistic as possible.

8. Once you feel like that step is complete, bring your awareness back to the present, and with your eyes still shut, start to think about what steps you will need to take in the next few days that will help you move closer to achieving your goal.

9. Take a few more deep breaths in order to ground yourself to the present before opening your eyes. Now, before you forget, write down a list of steps that you need to take in order to achieve your goal or begin to write down your experience in your journal, so you don't forget.

10. In this last step, you will focus on taking action and staying focused. Make sure that you are doing something that brings you closer to achieving your goal on a daily basis.

Use this meditation and visualization technique once a week after you first complete the steps. By doing this once a week, it helps you continue to move forward towards your end goal and help you bring your vision into real life. Seeing is believing, so using your mind and meditation, you are able to create the best future that you have imagined for yourself.

# Chapter 8: Master Self-Discipline

n the previous chapter, you learned numerous ips on how to increase your self-control and liscipline alongside with visualization and neditation techniques that can help increase rour overall skills and discipline. In this chapter, ve will take it one step further and talk about iome next-level tips that can make the previous ips learned even more effective. We will also talk about self-discipline and its relationship and iffects on anxiety. If you are someone that requently feels anxious regarding all your action tems, this is a good chapter for you to pay extra attention to.

## Next Level Tips

Remember, **motivation** is generated AFTER rou begin a task and not before. It creates a inowball effect that motivates you to complete nore and more tasks once you get started. There s no use sitting around waiting until you 'feel motivated' because that won't happen until you actually begin your task.

In order to create motivation and inspiration at a general level, you must have goals that you are truly passionate about. If you have goals that don't spark passion within yourself, you will struggle to justify giving up gratifications and 'free-time' to work on your goals. Choosing goals that really mean something to you is the first step you have to make to increase your self discipline.

Next, you must **be proactive**, responsible and exercise your self-esteem throughout the whole self-discipline process. Be proactive in the sense of preventing yourself from being exposed to gratifications so you don't have to waste your willpower turning it down.

We talked about this a few times earlier in the book. For instance, if you are trying to hit a financial goal and you know you have a bad habit of online shopping, put your credit cards away or have a family member keep them aside for you to prevent yourself from splurging when you see online sales. This is much more effective than forcing yourself to turn down a shopping opportunity when it is right in front of you.

Next, exercise **responsibility**. Having a goal that you are passionate about helps you do this automatically. If one of your goals is to save up money to help with your child's future college tuition, this will generate emotion and responsibility within you. Having a goal that truly means something and is good-natured can help you grow your responsibility skills.

In addition, growing your self-discipline not only helps you accomplish more goals in your life, but it also helps you grow your self-esteem. If you are someone right now that is struggling with self-esteem, focusing your energy and time into achieving goals will help build confidence within yourself. By showing yourself that you can do anything as long as you stay organized, proactive, and dedicated, you are fueling yourself with more self-confidence that will better your self-image.

*If you are interested in gaining better confidence and overcoming your insecurities, I wrote a book on the subject that you can find on Amazon. Go to the last page of this book and you will find the direct link.*

Since everyone is different, there are **different ways** to tackle all your daily action items. Some people like to get the hardest task out of the way so they have peace of mind later on, whilst others struggle to find the motivation to complete their hardest task so they start with the easiest first. There isn't a set of instructions for this, do some self-reflection and decide what works best for you. For me, I like to get the ball rolling by completing a couple of easy tasks first in the morning so I can get the juices flowing and motivation running.

Starting with a big and hard task right at the beginning of the day can create a lot of anxiety for someone. In fact, we shouldn't even be planning large tasks for ourselves. We need to always break them down into smaller ones in order to make them much easier to deal with. For most people, it's easier to complete 5 small tasks in a day than to complete 1 large one. This creates anxiety for those that are prone to it, which we will get into shortly.

**Sharing your goals** with other people helps build accountability. I mentioned this earlier in the book in the form of examples. For instance, if you are looking to get into better physical shape, find a work out buddy and have them meet you at the gym in the morning for workouts. You are much less likely to stand-up your friend this way.

Otherwise, with no one waiting for you at the gym on a rainy morning, you are very likely to skip your work out to get an extra hour of sleep in the morning. For goals that are possible, include a partner or a buddy to create accountability. Simply stop 'trying' to go to the gym and just do it. Put prevention measures in place and just get it done. Remember, when it becomes a habit, it no longer feels as hard and doesn't use up as much of your willpower as before.

Lastly, self-discipline helps relieve anxiety. When people have numerous tasks looming over their heads, it increases their chance of procrastinating which then causes anxiety as tasks begin to be overdue and it gets harder and harder to complete them. If you are someone who is prone to anxiety and is often anxious about the things they have to do, improving your self-discipline is a great way to overcome it.

**Break down big tasks** into smaller ones, so they're more manageable. Schedule them accordingly in a way that makes sense for your time. Prevent obstacles rather than dealing with them as you are faced with them. Exert your perseverance when you do face failures because you know it's just a part of the process. You can change your entire mindset regarding getting things done by simply building new habits and being proactive.

## Dealing With Setbacks and Develop a Growth Mindset

At this point in the book, I want to put a more focus on dealing with setbacks whilst developing and maintaining a growth mindset. The one thing that sets most people back from reaching their goals is not knowing how to deal with failures and adversity. We talked about this a handful of times earlier in the book, but I want to further emphasize this; failure is a part of the process. Don't fool yourself by believing that you won't face failure along the way. Everybody does, it's a part of the process. The difference between people who find success and those who don't is simply that those who did were able to learn from their failures, grow, and overcome it.

When you are faced with adversity, you must **forgive yourself** for any mistakes you have made and move forward. Famous snowboarder Mark McMorris, a multi-gold medal Olympian made a huge mistake that nearly cost him his life while snowboarding. Most people may have ended their athletic career right then and there

155

in fear for their life. However, he persevered healed, went through physiotherapy until he was well again.

This resulted in him winning more gold medals than ever before and is one of the most renowned athletes in the world. I hope that you never have to go through a life-threatening experience, but the point I'm trying to get across is that failures and mistakes are a part of the journey. Separate yourself from it and keep moving forward. Do what you can to grow and heal so you can come back stronger than before.

The **'growth mindset'** is a term that was coined by Carol Dweck who is a renowned professor at multiple universities including Columbia University, Harvard University and the University of Illinois. Her research with Angela Lee Duckworth stated that intelligence is not a key indicator of success. In fact, they believed that success depends on whether or not the person has a growth mindset. A fixed mindset is when a person believes that their intelligence and skills are a fixed trait. They have what they have and that's it.

This makes the person highly concerned with what skills and intelligence they currently have, and they do not focus on what they can gain. Therefore, their activities are limited to the capacity that they think they have. However, those with growth mindsets understand that skills and intelligence is something that can be developed and learned throughout the course of their life. This can be done through education, training, or simply just even passion. They understand that their brain is a muscle that can be 'worked out' to grow stronger.

Knowing this, it is important that you employ a growth mindset. Every single skill you have and your intelligence can be improved by putting in the effort to do so. Famous public figures of success like Oprah Winfrey, Steve Jobs and Bill Gates all employed a growth mindset by overcoming every obstacle that got in the way. Rather than succumbing to defeat, they worked and discovered innovative ways to overcome previous failures and found success at the end.

Think about what mindset you have right now. If you already have a growth mindset, you simply need to continue practicing it while being proactive about avoiding obstacles and overcoming failures. If you think you are someone with a fixed mindset, change it right now. Believe me when I tell you that intelligence and skills can be improved upon with time and hard work.

If you don't believe me, just try it. Pick a random skill. This could be knitting, programming, jogging or anything that can be learned. Set goals for yourself and begin learning something new. If you are able to take something that you have zero skill in and become proficient in it, you have just proved to yourself that growth mindsets are real and fixed mindsets only hold you back from success.

# The Final Challenge: Achieve Your Long Term Goals

In the last subchapter in this book, I want to emphasize the importance of achieving long term goals by resisting immediate wants and instant gratification. In order to do this, we must be able to **think in a long-term manner** and not a short-term one. Self-discipline is what allows people to resist temptation to support goals that will truly impact them in the future. Before certain tasks become habits, we have to persevere through every temptation using pure grit. However, a more effective solution is simply to avoid facing temptation where possible.

Angela Duckworth is a grit guru who talks about perseverance in her research studies back in 2016. She talks about how a person must have a passion for their long-term goals. Her study found that 'the achievement of different goals entails not only talent but also a sustained and focused application of talent over time', in other words, the practice of self-discipline. In this case, it is crucial that we **practice our grit** or otherwise known as our willpower in order to resist temptations that we will 100% be faced with.

Moreover, natural talent doesn't necessarily mean immediate success. Even the most naturally talented person won't be able to achieve anything if they don't apply their talent frequently. By practicing skills related to your long-term goal, you are making it easier for yourself over time by turning them into habits that will help you achieve your long-term goal.

A good example that a lot of people can relate to is striving to become debt-free. In our society in the present day, millions of people are crippled by student debt, credit card debt, mortgage loans and many other types of debt. If one of your goals is to become debt-free so you can start saving for a comfortable retirement, you must start building the skills and habits for it.

Those who simply say "I'm just bad with money!" or "I just love shopping too much!" are employing a fixed mindset where they are making assumptions about themselves regarding their inability to save money. Throw that mindset away and turn it into a **growth mindset**. Change negative phrases into positive ones such as "I've been bad with money in the past but I am going to learn to be more responsible with it" or "I love shopping but from now on I will budget for it instead".

In this example, people must build better spending habits by practicing different actions until it becomes a habit. They must also proactively create preventative measures that will stop them from spending money needlessly. For starters, you can **break down your long-term big goal into smaller ones**. If you are $50,000 in debt, break it down into paying off $10,000 each year over five years. Then break it down further, that's $833 per month. Then, break it down ever FURTHER, that's $208 per week.

All of a sudden, saving $208 per week sounds a lot more manageable than saving $50,000. Next, place preventative measures in order to avoid temptations that you know you always succumb to. If you enjoy going out for drinks on a Friday night, invite friends over to have a few drinks at your house instead, so you don't have to pay crazy bar prices.

If you tend to overspend your money, place a limit on your bank card so you can't spend your money needlessly. If you are an avid online shopper, get rid of your credit card altogether, or have a friend or family member safe-keep it for you. This will reduce the amount you need to use your willpower and leave you with more energy to work on other goals.

Once you get the ball rolling and it's been three consecutive weeks of saving $208, you should be feeling motivated to keep going. Try to increase that number if you can. Open a locked savings account to put that $208 in every week so you can't access that money even if you wanted to. Or even better, set up an auto-deposit to automatically transfer $208 every week into your savings account so you don't even have to think about it. All of a sudden, your $50,000 goal has turned into one that happens habitually whilst requiring minimal willpower.

Create a customized plan that fits whatever goal you are looking to reach. Avoid temptations while practicing your willpower so you can actually reach your long-term goal and not only dream of it.

Photo by Thao Le Hoang on Unsplash

# Conclusion

I first want you to give yourself a pat on the back for exercising your self-discipline by learning and reading about all the content in this book. That is a great first step you took by learning more about self-discipline in order to reach your long-term goals. Most people have varied misconceptions regarding self-discipline, I hope that the content of this book has changed your mind regarding this topic and you now understand that having the right mindset and preparations, can help you find success.

We covered a lot of topics throughout this book. We first started by learning about why it's necessary to improve one's self-discipline. We then learned about the expected benefits and how self-discipline can improve your life in many aspects, including personal, business and relationships. Next, we dove into the depths of the science behind self-discipline. We learned about willpower and studied multiple case studies that proved that willpower is a resource that can be depleted.

We then learned about habits and how they do not require willpower. We also learned about Basal Ganglia, which is the area of our brain that plays a part in generating habits. Throughout the book, habits are mentioned as a great technique to get tasks done without needing to draw from your willpower resource. Next, we learned about how people with higher self-control tend to be happier than those without. We learned that self-discipline brings more satisfaction to a person's life along with success.

Towards the middle of this book, we spent some time learning about failures. We learned that they are part of the process of gaining success and that the only way to reach goals is to expect failures and learn to move past them. We also learned about how low self-discipline can cause more failures and how to mitigate those causes.

We spent a lot of time in the next chapter learning step-by-step how to increase self-discipline. In addition, we learned about two different techniques; visualization and mindfulness meditation. These tools are here to help you reinforce your self-discipline and to grow whatever skill that will help you reach your goals.

In the last chapter, we learned more next-level tips that are a combination of proactiveness, responsibility, self-esteem and anxiety relief. These tips will help you take your self-discipline to a new level once you've got the basic downs. At the end of this book, we spent more time learning about setbacks and developing a growth mindset. Both of these topics are important in order for a person to achieve their long-term goals.

By the time you got to these chapters, I wanted you to have **two main takeaways**. First, I want you to know that a growth mindset is necessary for success and self-discipline. Without it, you remain stagnant and unable to learn and grow. No one can find success this way.

Second, I want you to understand that failures and temptations are everywhere around us. We can do our very best to prevent and avoid them as much as we can, but at the end of the day, we must exert our willpower in the face of temptation in order to reach our long-term goals. Employ goals that you are passionate about so willpower comes more naturally to you.

The next step now is to simply apply these methodologies, tips, and concepts into your reality. Make good goals for yourself that you're passionate about. Break it down into smaller ones and prevent temptation. I promise you that once you get the ball rolling, you'll be able to accomplish more than you have ever imagined.

## *Final words:*

Here we are... ;-)

"Self-Discipline Mastery" is over.

Thank you again for having read this book.

If you are serious about the will to improve your self-discipline skills, I recommend reading this book a few times and starting to put into practice everything you have learned in this book. This way you will quickly overcome bad habits, lead your life to higher happiness and satisfaction and achieve all the goals that you've always wanted to achieve!

If you prefer to use the digital version to help you organize an action plan:

**https://www.amazon.com/dp/B0825WYM5Q**

If you prefer to use the audiobook version, it will be available soon.

I wish you the very best of luck with the achievement of your goals!!

# *Did you enjoy this guide?*

If you enjoyed this book, it would be awesome if you could leave a quick review on Amazon. Your feedback is much appreciated and I would love to hear from you. You can do it right here... ;-)

## **Leave a Review on Amazon**

Thanks so much!!

## More books by Dalton McKay:

**Self-Esteem Workbook: A Practical Guide to Help You Overcome Self-Doubt and Insecurity, Gain Better Confidence, and Find Your Inner Strength. Discover Your Hidden Potential and Change Your Life in 30 Days. (Link)**

*More books by Dalton McKay:*

Effective Communication Skills: How to Talk to Anyone. A Practical Guide to Boost Your Conversation and Writing Skills in the Workplace, Improve Charisma and Build Healthy Interpersonal Relationships (Link)

## More books by Dalton McKay:

**Overcome Social Anxiety: A Practical Guide to Symptoms, Causes and Solutions. Discover How YOU Can Easily Cope With Panic Attacks, Phobias, and Depression and How to Improve YOUR Social Skills. (Link)**

CPSIA information can be obtained
at www.ICGtesting.com
Printed in the USA
BVHW091240161120
593417BV00008B/831

9 781801 209